www.wadsworth.com

www.wadsworth.com is the World Wide Web site for Wadsworth and is your direct source to dozens of online resources.

At *www.wadsworth.com* you can find out about supplements, demonstration software, and student resources. You can also send email to many of our authors and preview new publications and exciting new technologies.

www.wadsworth.com
Changing the way the world learns®

THE WADSWORTH COLLEGE SUCCESS SERIES

Connect College to Career

A Student's Guide to

Work and Life Transitions

PAUL I. HETTICH
Barat College of DePaul University

CAMILLE HELKOWSKI
Loyola University Chicago

THOMSON

WADSWORTH

Australia • Canada • Mexico • Singapore • Spain
United Kingdom • United States

THOMSON

WADSWORTH

Executive Manager: Carolyn Merrill
Technology Project Manager: Joe Gallagher
Advertising Project Manager: Linda Yip
Project Manager, Editorial Production:
  Candace Chen
Print Buyer: Emma Claydon
Permissions Editor: Kiely Sexton

Production Service: Peggy Francomb,
  Shepherd, Inc.
Copy Editor: Colleen Yonda
Cover Designer: Laurie Anderson
Cover Image: © Jason Reed/PhotoDisc
Compositor: Shepherd Inc.
Text/Cover Printer: Webcom

Printed in Canada
1 2 3 4 5 6 7 08 07 06 05 04

For more information about our products,
contact us at:
Thomson Learning Academic Resource Center
1-800-423-0563
For permission to use material from this text or
product, submit a request online at
http://www.thomsonrights.com.
Any additional questions about permissions
can be submitted by email to
thomsonrights@thomson.com.

Library of Congress Control Number:
2003115875

ISBN: 0-534-62582-7

Thomson Wadsworth
10 Davis Drive
Belmont, CA 94002-3098
USA

Asia
Thomson Learning
5 Shenton Way #01-01
UIC Building
Singapore 068808

Australia/New Zealand
Thomson Learning
102 Dodds Street
Southbank, Victoria 3006
Australia

Canada
Nelson
1120 Birchmount Road
Toronto, Ontario M1K 5G4
Canada

Europe/Middle East/Africa
Thomson Learning
High Holborn House
50/51 Bedford Row
London WC1R 4LR
United Kingdom

Latin America
Thomson Learning
Seneca, 53
Colonia Polanco
11560 Mexico D.F.
Mexico

Spain/Portugal
Paraninfo
Calle Magallanes, 25
28015 Madrid, Spain

To all who must confront transitions caused by war,
including Paul, Phil, Tom, and Dustin

To Bob, Becca, Matthew, Robyn, Eric, Andrew, and Meg—
who inspire my life and work

Brief Contents

Contents

Preface

Over a million students are awarded a baccalaureate degree from American colleges and universities each year. Most graduates enter the workforce with high expectations and satisfactory academic preparation, but most are unprepared for the organizational culture, tasks, and adjustments they encounter. Too many students assume that mastering the coursework of their academic major prepares them for work and life. Too many students assume that the interview and resume-writing skills they acquire, along with their work experiences, are sufficient for a smooth transition into the workplace. However, these suppositions are incorrect. The nature of work in the American economy has changed so drastically during recent decades that traditional assumptions relating college to career have been challenged. Furthermore, graduates continue their psychosocial growth and search for an identity influenced by changes in societal and life-style trends. The transition from college to life and work is unnecessarily painful for many individuals. *Connect College to Career: A Student's Guide to Work and Life Transitions* serves as a "red alert" for students; it encourages them to recognize that transition is the central issue and consciously begin the process *before* graduation.

GOALS

The goals of this book are to

- inform undergraduates about personal and professional issues of transition they will encounter after college,

- provide a conceptual anchor for understanding and interpreting transition issues, and

- recommend courses of action during the junior and senior years that facilitate transition to life and workplace.

AUDIENCE

We wrote this book for

- undergraduate juniors and seniors enrolled in career planning, capstone, and internship courses, as well as those independent learners who read it on their own time; and

- teachers, supervisors, career counselors, and student affairs professionals who recognize the importance of helping students hurtle across the exciting but often ominous space between college and the reality of their careers and lives.

ORGANIZATION

We begin by explaining the stages of transition and introduce the book's content with a self-assessment scale. In chapter 2 we examine student preparedness, promote the importance of jobs, and summarize a perspective for understanding new employee learning tasks. Students acquire knowledge about psychosocial (chapter 3) and cognitive development (chapter 4) dimensions that influence transition. We challenge readers to expand their understanding of intelligence (chapter 5) and examine the influence of motivation and learning on performance in college and work settings (chapter 6). Subsequently we explore relationships within personal, work, and community contexts (chapter 7) and the connections between academic majors and career and life choices (chapter 8). We conclude with a review of main themes readers can apply to daily living and a positive message about achieving optimal experiences (chapter 9). The immediate needs of the reader may direct their interests in a different order such as beginning with chapter 8 or chapter 3. We wrote the chapters in a way that permits jumping in and out of the material at will.

LEARNER OUTCOMES

As a result of reading *Connect College to Career: A Student's Guide to Work and Life Transitions,* students should be able to

- recognize that college and professional workplaces differ in their perspectives on performance, learning, and organizational culture;

- understand social and cognitive developmental processes that shape the ways they view themselves, their work, and their world;

- describe several perspectives on what it means to act intelligently;
- understand how motivational and learning processes direct actions;
- understand the nature of relationships in work and life settings;
- critically examine issues that help them identify themes for guiding career and life choices; and
- actively apply the concepts and suggestions during their remaining academic terms and after college.

FEATURES

Connect College to Career: A Student's Guide to Work and Life Transitions is unique in its application of social science, student affairs, and career counseling concepts to preparing for work and life transitions. We incorporate theory and research on psychosocial, cognitive and student development, career planning, and organizational behavior; we use student experiences to support conceptual frameworks. We encourage the reader to become actively involved with the material several ways.

- Material is supported by student cases.
- Exercises elicit immediate application of ideas.
- All chapters contain practical recommendations.
- End-of-chapter Journal Starters stimulate further examination and application of concepts.

"I find the great thing in this world is not so much where we stand, as in what direction we are moving: To reach the port of heaven, we must sail sometimes with the wind and sometimes against it — but we must sail, and not drift, nor lie at anchor." *Oliver Wendell Holmes, Sr.*

ACKNOWLEDGMENTS

Although our two names appear on the cover, we could not have completed this project without the assistance of several individuals. At Wadsworth Publishing we express our gratitude to the professional staff for transforming a manuscript into an attractive volume. Specifically, we thank Carolyn Merrill and Candace Chen at Wadsworth, and Peggy Francomb at Shepherd, Inc.

We are grateful to Christine Anderson, Marcia Baxter Magolda, Charlotte Briggs, Jacque Elder, Mary Taylor Johnson, Dee Konrad, Lindsay O'Brien, Joe Reaves, and Maureen Smith who performed critical readings of draft chapters and offered valuable suggestions, and to Jerry Cleland who shared his technical expertise. In addition, we appreciated the helpful comments and insights of Suzanne Houston, Jon Keil, Jodee Kelly, America Martinez, Michael Myers, and Jennifer Schmitz.

We acknowledge and thank our reviewers whose efforts made this manuscript the book it is: Linda Garlinger, Missouri Western State College; Paul Gore, Southern Illinois University—Carbondale; Tracy Hakala, James Madison University; William Holmes, Lamar University; Kenneth Jackson; Faye Johnson, Middle Tennessee State University; Jason Krupp, St. Petersburg College; Dana Levy, Lynn University; Carolyn Manley, Moraine Valley Community College; Sydney Perry, Jr., Old Dominion University; Bruce Peterson, Sonoma State University; Brian Riedesel, The University of Utah; Wendy Stubbs, University of South Dakota; and Andrew Watters, Penn State Erie, The Behrend College.

Paul Hettich is grateful to DePaul University for providing resources that enabled him to coauthor this book. Camille Helkowski thanks the staff of Loyola University Chicago's Internship & Career Center for their on-going encouragement and their support of her writing efforts.

1

Transitions, Expectations, and the Journey Ahead

"The best part of our lives we pass on counting on what is to come."

WILLIAM HAZLITT

Life is a journey, and college is one of its most exciting destinations for those fortunate to travel there. College is a time of freedom, exploration, fun, frustration, hard work, and growth (often, in that order!). Toward the end, you are filled with anticipation and expectation of the future—how to use your education and experiences to make your way in the world. Soon you will journey from college to new destinations. What will your passage be like, and what are your expectations of the changes ahead? Is British essayist William Hazlitt correct? The purposes of this chapter are to explore the meaning of transition and assess some of your beliefs and expectations about life after college.

WHAT IS A TRANSITION?

We begin in a manner familiar to college students—defining key terms. According to *Webster's Third New International Dictionary of the English Language Unabridged* (Gove 1993), transition is "a passage or movement from one state, condition, or place to another." You have experienced many passages: from child to adult, elementary to high school to college, dependent to less dependent, and naïve to critical thinker, to name a few. More passages lie ahead. According to Tom Smith (2003), transition to adulthood is common to all societies throughout history. Not only does transition differ among cultures and time periods, in America it has changed somewhat from previous generations. For instance, the median age at marriage for women rose from 20 in 1960 to 25 in 2000, and the legal age for being tried as an adult has been lowered in most states.

Smith (2003) surveyed about 1400 American adults using the 2002 General Social Survey (GSS) to determine the importance of seven youth-to-adult transitions. Respondents (about 1350) maintained that it is "extremely," "quite," or "somewhat" important for young persons to complete their education (97%), achieve financial independence (97%), obtain full-time employment (95%), support a family (94%), not live with parents (82%), get married (55%), and have a child (52%). If you experience pressures from family or friends to move through these passages, remember that their views are shared by a strong majority of adults.

When this sample was asked when these transitions should occur, the mean ages reported were: twenty-one for achieving financial independence, not living with parents, and obtaining full-time employment; 22 for completing your education; 25 for supporting a family; and 26 for marriage and parenthood. Less than 17% of the sample believe that financial independence, living away from parents, and full-time employment should wait until a person is 25 years or older; only 22% believe completing education should wait until 25 or older. Some differences existed within the sample as a function of age, education, ethnic group, gender, marital status, and race regarding certain transitions, but it is beyond the scope of this chapter to report further details. Three important observations emerge from Smith's survey.

- American young people are expected to pass through several important transitions before society regards them as adults.
- Most adults believe these transitions should occur by age 26.
- The transitions are expected to normally occur in a short five-year period between 21 and 26 years of age.

You expect your experiences and education to prepare you well for these transitions. Yet, some of you are thinking you are over 21 and have yet to complete one passage. Do not permit the survey results to increase the pressures you already experience as you approach graduation, for *you* will choose (whether externally or internally motivated) when (or if) you pass through these transitions. Still, you should view this information as a "red alert" about issues you face now and in the future. Your transition from college will consist of the knowledge and experiences you accumulate as you pass from being a student to your new endeavors, whether it is a job, further education, or other activities. Finally, do not view transition only in terms of time, knowledge, changes, and experiences.

William Bridges is a former English professor who "transitioned" from the academic world during the 1970s to become a leading business consultant, author, and expert on transition. He distinguishes change from transition: Change refers to events and situations that occur, whereas transition is your particular experiences with these events (Bridges 1994). Beginning college, a new job, or a new relationship represents a change from earlier circumstances; your particular experiences with these events represent a transition or passage from previous to new situations. In *Managing Transitions: Making the Most of Change* (2003), Bridges describes three overlapping phases or processes of transition.

- In the *ending phase,* an individual breaks away from the old identity or ways of doing things.
- In the *neutral zone,* a person is between two ways or habits of doing or being. The old ways are gone, but new beliefs, attitudes, or habits have not been firmly established yet.
- In the *new beginning,* an individual is productive and goal-oriented in the new ways and possesses a new identity that corresponds to the new situation.

"Because transition is a process by which people unplug from an old world and plug into a new world, we can say that transition starts with an ending and finishes with a beginning" (Bridges 2003, p.5).

As you reflect on the transition processes, it is tempting to conclude that; (1) graduation is your disengagement from the way things were in college (your ending); (2) the time between graduation and your new work is the neutral zone; and (3) the new beginning occurs the first week of your new life.

Not really!

Instead, we want you to reexamine the notion of endings and neutral zones. View graduation as the ceremonial conclusion of the ending phase, not the ending itself. Graduation is the point of physical departure from your institution with diploma in hand and the inspiring words of the commencement speakers mostly forgotten. We want you to *begin* your ending much sooner. Our primary message is this: *When you carefully plan and construct your remaining academic terms and activities as essential components of your ending phase, the neutral zone and new beginning will likely be productive and satisfying.* If you are a junior or senior, we want you to reexamine certain beliefs and attitudes that became well established during the 16 or 17 years of your formal education and consider new perspectives. You cannot disengage completely because there are courses and other requirements to fulfill before graduation. However, your disengagement from college should include a search for how to connect, integrate, and apply your experiences and resources to your future plans *now,* while you are still in college, while there is time in your schedule to use the advice we offer. Too many graduates discover too late that they should have used their last years of college differently. If you talk with recent college graduates, many will quickly tell you what they should have done differently.

Why should it take so long to disengage from college? In Bridges' *neutral zone,* the individual has not yet shed the old ways of doing things. During seemingly endless years of formal education, students become *conditioned* to learn in a culture dominated by specified student-teacher roles, expectations, reward structures (grades), and repetitive schedules of academic terms and class meetings. The subject matter may differ from term-to-term, but the procedures for learning remain essentially unchanged. It is very difficult to extinguish highly engrained expectations, attitudes, and habits established before and during college and then substitute new ones, especially when you encounter a very different world that demands rapid adjustment to its changing modes of operations.

Most graduates enter the workplace assuming that the expectations, attitudes, and behaviors that worked in college automatically apply in the new setting. Some slip comfortably into a new organization and pass through the neutral zone in a few months, but many discover that the neutral zone is a "hot zone"—challenging and often painful—and need one or more years to reach a new beginning. In chapter 3, Sharon Daloz Parks labels such painful experiences as a "shipwreck." Bridges views the neutral zone as a limbo, a psychological no-man's-land between the old and new ways of doing things. The astute graduate may be aware that the way things were done in college may not be appropriate, but is not sure which attitudes and habits should be retained and which set aside because the new work setting contains so many uncertainties. It is important that you know about the neutral zone so that you do not try to rush through it (and become frustrated), escape from it (and change jobs—turnover is common among recent graduates), or miss opportunities to apply your interests and skills creatively early in your career (Bridges 2003).

At the end of the neutral zone is the new beginning when individuals have established a new identity compatible with the new organization; they are comfortable with their new role and productive. "Letting go, repatterning, and making a new beginning: together these processes reorient and renew people when things are changing all around them" (Bridges 2003, p. 9).

The transition from college is only one of life's important passages. You survived transitions to high school and college, to jobs, and, perhaps, to living in new places or cultures. Chances are, the challenges those transitions posed will be matched or exceeded by others, such as changes in important relationships, parenthood, health problems, career challenges, and responding to crises. As individuals, we cannot always control change, but we can try to prepare for the transitions that change causes.

WHAT ARE YOUR EXPECTATIONS?

Throughout your education, family, friends, teachers and others said that success is very difficult without a college degree. You are investing at least four years of your life (more if you work full-time) and untold effort, emotional energy, and various resources. You study with learned instructors, read more books than you knew possible, write numerous papers, and sharpen your thinking skills Often you give up free time, social life, and extracurricular activities—sometimes everything—to earn the degree. At the end of college you may owe tens of thousands of dollars in loans, and some loan payments are due only months after graduation. To justify your many hardships, naturally you *expect* a good job, a satisfying career, and a comfortable life-style. Why shouldn't you have high expectations? Isn't the good life what the degree promises, at least implicitly?

Your expectations about the value of your college education may be realistic, but expectations pertaining to your next work environment should cause you concern. What specific beliefs, attitudes, and habits that you developed during college will be most useful to you during the first year or two after college? Your belief that intelligence and a strong G.P.A. are highly appreciated? Your attitude that people without a college degree will be boring? Your habit of sticking with your beliefs in the face of all opposition? Stop reading now and pause to consider such issues. Then create a short list of your expectations on the lines below.

The Question: What particular ideas, attitudes, and behaviors about others, my environment, and myself do I expect to benefit me most during my transition?

_____

_____

_____

_____

_____

When we ask supervisors and employers about the most challenging issues that face recent college graduates, most cite graduates' unrealistic expectations, including expectations about promotion, salary, and their readiness to work in a "real" job. Were any of these issues in your list? Some graduates enter the work place with a realistic understanding of what lies ahead, they adapt successfully, and they advance. However, too many graduates discover, to their chagrin, major discrepancies between what they expected and what they found in the workplace. We hope this does not happen to you, but it might. Remember: The organization that hires you or the graduate or professional school that admits you also has high expectations or it would not have accepted your application.

This book addresses several issues that may help you reduce—or at least understand—the discrepancies between your expectations and your transition experiences. As an introduction to topics covered in the next eight chapters, we want you to complete the self-assessment scale below by marking in the left margin of the item the number or term that best describes your response. Then compare your responses to the commentary that follows the scale.

Strongly Agree	Agree	Neither Agree or Disagree	Disagree	Strongly Disagree
1	2	3	4	5

_____ 1. I believe that the adjustment from college to post-college work environments is often a major obstacle for recent graduates.

_____ 2. I expect the knowledge and skills I gained from my academic major will be the best predictor of my preparedness for a job.

_____ 3. I expect the primary challenge I will face as a newly hired college grad is to master the specific task knowledge and skills required by the position.

_____ 4. By the time I graduate from college, my sense of identity and social-psychological development will be nearly complete.

_____ 5. Once I have chosen a set of values and a career path, there is no point in questioning these commitments.

_____ 6. Since I have a strong life and career plan while still in college, I can avoid the typical "who-am-I-and-what-do-I-want-to-do" graduation crisis.

_____ 7. As students progress from freshmen to seniors, they encounter more uncertainties regarding their beliefs about the world.

_____ 8. Courses that promote discussion and group projects may facilitate higher levels of thinking better than straight lecture courses.

_____ 9. Service learning and part-time jobs may provide students with an experiential complement to course work, but they cannot teach you how to function in settings that require sophisticated levels of knowing.

_____10. I expect the best predictor of success in the workplace is the G.P.A.

_____11. I believe analytical and problem solving intelligence is almost always more important in the workplace than creative or emotional processes.

_____12. While I am adjusting to the demands of a new job, I will also have to develop competencies in navigating the numerous dimensions of independent living.

_____13. In the long run, it really makes no difference whether I am motivated by external sources such as family and teachers or whether my motivation comes from within.

_____14. I believe what other people do in their job and the rewards they receive for doing it should have no bearing in my motivation to work.

_____15. In general, some people learn how to operate in their world primarily by doing, others by observing, and still others by analyzing.

_____16. Adjusting to the differences between college and post-college relationships can be a daunting task without the support of a mentor.

_____17. Although employers consider the ability to be an effective member of a team an essential quality for employees to possess, there are few meaningful opportunities to develop these skills during college.

_____18. College has given me a community of like-minded friends much too solid to be affected by graduation.

_____19. I expect the most important factor for determining my career path is my undergraduate major.

_____20. A good career plan incorporates my family background, personality traits, and makes room for unanticipated changes along my path.

_____21. During my senior year of college, I should begin the career-planning process by writing a resume.

We hope this exercise stimulated your thinking about transition issues. While there are no absolutely correct or incorrect answers to the scale items, evidence exists to support particular positions discussed below. Your responses were based on a five-point scale, but, to be expedient, we will indicate our answer to each item with a simple "Agree" or "Disagree."

Chapter 2 From College to Corporate Culture:
You're a Freshman Again!

Adjusting to the differences between college and post-college work settings does pose a major problem for most graduates, especially those with little or no significant work experience (item 1: agree). The discrepancies are the result of contrasting organizational cultures and learning processes, not simply academic preparation. Chapter 2 explores differences between college and the workplace. Although the knowledge and skills you gained from your major are important, they may not be the best predictor of success in your career (item 2: disagree). Why? In part, because learning a new job includes far more than mastering specific job tasks, information, and skills (item 3: disagree). Chapter 2 describes a four-stage taxonomy of new employee learning tasks, the last of which is the mastering of tasks.

Chapter 3 Coming of Age: Young Adult Development

Human development does not end with college graduation; it is, in fact, a lifelong process (item 4, disagree). During college you sharpen your sense of identity, personal values, and commitment to an occupation. In order to make a committed choice in these areas, it is necessary to ask questions, to be a seeker, perhaps to experience a crisis of faith. In short, it is necessary to "not know" for a while (item 5, disagree). Although many students try to avoid "not knowing," it is a critical part of making good choices about yourself and your work (item 6, disagree).

Chapter 4 Cognitive Development During and After College: What You Should Know About Knowing

Do you remember that years ago you often believed the answers to most questions could be found in a textbook or by asking your instructors or some other authority? Over the years you learned that multiple perspectives exist on most issues, knowledge is often uncertain, and authorities can be wrong (item 7, agree). Changes in the process of knowing occur in different stages or levels during college, but studies suggest that higher levels of knowing do not increase appreciably until after college. However, courses that promote discussion and group projects as well as experience-based activities can facilitate development of higher levels of knowing (item 8, agree; item 9, disagree).

Chapter 5 Intelligence Revisited: What It Really Means to Be Smart

Most of us have been conditioned since our first years of school to think of intelligence in terms of grades and test scores. Yet some experts argue that academic and analytic measures of intelligence, although essential, are overemphasized in education at the expense of under-valuing creative, practical, and emotional forms of intelligence (items 10 and 11: disagree) that are equally or more important. Chapter 5 examines these issues so you can expand your thinking about what it really means to be smart after you write your last final exam. As many organizations focus on employee competence, we will review one model of competences that has gained recent attention. Not all competences are job-related, however. If you never lived independently, you will want to quickly develop non-job-related competence in understanding issues such as insurance, credit, buying cars, and apartment living (item 12, agree). Space does not permit us to address these issues in depth, but we identify resources you can check.

Chapter 6 Motivation and Learning: Principles That Work When You Do

Chapter 6 summarizes motivation and learning concepts derived from research and practices in organizational settings that can facilitate your best performance in whatever work you choose. It is essential that you understand the factors that motivate you during college if you want your motivational energy to work for you later on. Your will to learn and do well should come from within yourself, not from outside sources (teachers, family, supervisors) that cannot follow you wherever you go (item 13, disagree). We will introduce you to three workplace theories of motivation (goal setting, equity, and expectancy) to stimulate your thinking about this essential dimension of transition. For example, whether we want to admit it or not, there are times when other people's work levels and rewards strongly influence our desire to work (item 14, disagree). Many principles of learning that subtly influenced your behavior in school, such as operant learning (rewards and punishments) and imitation, are briefly examined in the context of work. According to Kolb's experiential learning cycle, some individuals generally learn by doing, others by observing, and still others by analyzing (item 15, agree). You should be aware of your preferred modes of learning and the way they could influence your professional and personal modes of acting.

Chapter 7 Relationships—at Home, at Work, in the Community

While shifts in relationships begin well before college ends, it may be hard to recognize them. After graduation, however, these changes are almost impossible to miss. College friends are often all over the map, and relationships at work are not forged overnight (item 16, agree). Your relationships and involvements during college have honed your interpersonal and team skills, but you must also learn the way your workplace operates (item 17, disagree). It is important to be aware of the "shifting sands" that are the hallmark of post-graduation relationships of all kinds and be willing to adjust your expectations of the old as well as be open to new possibilities (item 18, disagree).

Chapter 8 Working to Your Heart's Content

Declaring a major is only the beginning of the career-planning process (item 19, disagree). While it sets the stage, choosing your work is a complex and lengthy procedure. It is first necessary to know yourself—your values, skills, interests, personality preferences, impact of your family and community on your identity—in order to clarify your sense of "call" (item 20, agree). Once you have a sense of whom you want to become, you can begin researching, networking, and experiencing the world of work. Finally, it is time to incorporate job-search techniques (21, disagree).

Chapter 9 Looking Back and Moving Forward

Chapter 9 looks back. Transition is a passage from one condition to another; William Bridges maintains that it begins by disengaging from the old ways (an ending). If you want a successful transition to life and work, begin your ending now. We will review the main themes from each chapter and encourage you to actively incorporate them into your life *now* while you have the time and opportunities. To facilitate this process, we will create an "A List"—a To Do List of specific steps you can take to generate *awareness* and *action* for your disengagement while you complete your remaining requirements. Chapter 9 also looks forward. If you believe that college changed you, prepare for other life transformations in the years ahead as you continue to let go of some attitudes and habits and assume new ones, like a trapeze artist who reaches out through open space and grasps the bar that carries her or him to another dimension.

AND THE ANSWERS ARE . . .

The purpose of the self-assessment scale was to stimulate your thinking about transition issues as we summarized major topics in this book. The scale is not a validated instrument and does not have norms that permit you to compare your performance to that of others. However, when you compare your responses with ours, you receive general feedback about your knowledge of transition issues.

First, combine the "Strongly Agree"' with "Agree" responses and the "Strongly Disagree" with "Disagree" responses to create categories of Agree and Disagree and enter them below.

Item	Your Response	Ours
1.	_____	Agree
2.	_____	Disagree
3.	_____	Disagree
4.	_____	Disagree
5.	_____	Disagree
6.	_____	Disagree
7.	_____	Agree
8.	_____	Agree
9.	_____	Disagree
10.	_____	Disagree
11.	_____	Disagree
12.	_____	Agree
13.	_____	Disagree
14.	_____	Disagree
15.	_____	Agree
16.	_____	Agree
17.	_____	Disagree
18.	_____	Disagree
19.	_____	Disagree
20.	_____	Agree
21.	_____	Disagree

Count the number of items in which your response matches ours. If your responses agree with ours on at least 16 of the 21 (approximately 75%) items, congratulate yourself for having a good basic knowledge of transition issues. However, please do not return this book for a refund because we are confident that you will gain valuable insights in subsequent chapters. If fewer than

16 of your responses matched ours, then you are advised to *study* this book; it could be the difference between a successful or a poor transition.

As the first stage of your transition is an ending, we end this first chapter by returning to its beginning and William Hazlitt's comment, "The best part of our lives we pass on counting on what is to come." Is college the best part of your life, or is the best yet to come? Will you be ready for it?

JOURNAL STARTERS

Even good ideas can go in one ear and out the other if you do not reflect on what you learned or try to apply them. The purpose of journal writing is to encourage you to reflect and connect (Hettich 1990). Higher education researcher Alexander Astin (1999) is convinced that students' level of learning is directly related to their level of involvement in the learning activities. Consequently, at the end of each chapter, we provide a few journal starters that enable you to continue exploring the chapter's major ideas in a personally meaningful manner.

We suggest that you maintain a special notebook—the transition journal—apart from other notes you will take on the material. Begin each entry on a new page and enter the date. If you prefer, open a computer file entitled "Transition Journal" and type entries for each chapter. If you are using this book as part of a course, your instructor may assign certain Journal Starters as entries. Think about the topic and then write a page or two reflecting your thoughts. You may also elect to write an "open" entry on any topic of your choice that relates to course material. In chapter 4, you will learn that forming connections among ideas or between ideas and your experiences is one characteristic of higher level knowing. View the journal not as an assignment from us or from your instructor, but as a special opportunity to have a dialogue with yourself, the person who ultimately will become your best teacher, friend, and critic. Periodically review your journal entries and trace the development of your thoughts and growth. Enjoy!

1. William Bridges identifies three overlapping stages in transitions: an ending, a neutral zone, and a new beginning. Carefully review his definitions of each stage. Choose a significant transition that you experienced, e.g., relocation of residence, new school, new relationship, and write about the extent to which your transition fits in each of his stages.

2. Review the self-assessment scale you completed. Which of the answers we offered most surprised you? Why? Which topics are most important to you? Why?

3. What are the most significant insights you gained from reading this chapter? What concerns do you have about the meaning of the material?

REFERENCES

Astin, A. W. (1999). Involvement in Learning revisited: Lessons we have learned. *Journal of College Student Personnel* 40(5): 587–598.

Bridges, W. (1994). *Job shift: How to prosper in a workplace without jobs.* New York: Addison–Wesley.

Bridges, W. (2003). *Managing transitions: Making the most of change* (2nd Ed). Cambridge, MA: Perseus Books Group.

Gove, P. B. (Ed.). (1993). *Webster's Third New International Dictionary of the English Language Unabridged.* Springfield, MA: Merriam-Webster, Inc.

Hettich, P. (1990). Journal writing: Old fare or nouvelle cuisine? *Teaching of Psychology* 17: 36–39.

Smith, T. W. (2003). *Coming of age in 21st century America: Public attitudes towards the importance and timing of transitions to adulthood* (GSS Topical Report No. 35). Chicago: University of Chicago, National Opinion Research Center.

2

From College to Corporate Culture

You're a Freshman Again!

"On Sunday, the commencement speaker said I was one of the smartest people in America. Then, on Monday, I had to take a typing test."

RICHARD D. THAU

D oes the title of this chapter disturb you? Recognize that for most students the transition from school to their first full-time job is equivalent to becoming a freshman again.

- Once again, you begin a new chapter in your life as a new member of an organization.

- Your past achievements do not mean much to your supervisor and co-workers, many of whom had similar experiences.

- The strategies that helped you through college may not work because the workplace is a different environment.

- You will have to work harder because the demands are likely to be greater.

- Adapting to a new organizational culture can be intimidating.

An organization's culture refers to the expectations and beliefs that are manifested in its policies, practices, traditions, and ways people relate to each other. Chances are that most of you chose your current college or university in part because of its atmosphere, traditions, and distinctiveness. Just as your success in college depends partially on your compatibility with its culture, your ability to adapt to a new organization's culture will be a significant predictor of success.

The opening quotation from Richard Thau reflects his "extremely sobering" job-hunting experience after graduating from Haverford College (Lieber 1999). Subsequently, he and Jay Heflin combined their experiences with that of employment experts to write *Get It Together by 30* (1997), a career-planning and job-hunting guide for graduates. In this chapter, we will summarize what research studies say about the preparedness of students for the workplace, key differences between college and corporate working environments, the importance of work experience, and the tasks that new employees must master.

READY OR NOT?

Are college graduates prepared for the workplace? No and yes.

You are preparing for work that is structured differently from that of your grandfather's job and probably that of your mother's. According to William Bridges (1994), the rules of work have changed. Your grandfather may have been promised a job for life, but job security is gone; new graduates should expect to have multiple careers and work for several organizations. One of the new rules is that everyone is a contingency worker. People's jobs are contingent upon their productivity and not just in one assignment but in all of them. Consequently, the contemporary worker must deliberately create a mindset to think and act as a self-employed vendor, continually demonstrate (sell) the value of his or her skills and services, and view everyone in the organization as a customer. In short, *you are the salesperson of You, each day you are on the job.* In the past, job descriptions clearly defined what the employee did or did not have to do. However, the TIMJ ("This Isn't My Job") mindset of old has been replaced by expectations that employees cross boundaries and work collaboratively as members of diverse teams whose pay and promotions may hinge more on teamwork than on individual accomplishments (Bridges 1994). Yes, you *will* have a college degree—as will most persons competing for your job and the job you aspire to (provided it has not been outsourced or replaced by technology).

In her review of research conducted on the socialization of new employees, Debra Major (2000) concluded that individuals who enter high performance, dynamic organizations that compete in a global marketplace must demonstrate three types of abilities.

1. Flexibility and Adaptability In organizations where the job description and TIMJ attitude are considered dysfunctional, employees must cope with changes in work schedules, work processes and procedures, and coworkers. They need to be open to change, manage new work relationships, and develop skills needed to learn quickly and meet changing demands.

2. Continuous Learning and Self-Development Flexibility and adaptability require an appetite for continuous learning and the ability to deal with ambiguity. Employees are responsible for identifying their learning needs and the means to satisfy them. In short, employees must "learn their living." Yet, the prerequisite skills for thoughtful self-development are self-awareness, identity-exploration, and self-assessment, i.e., behaviors that represent Socrates' counsel to "know thyself." Chapter 3 addresses self-identity, chapter 5, emotional intelligence, and chapter 6, motivation. Finally, continuous personal and professional development enables you to collect the data you need to shape your career goals. Perhaps you can better understand the words you hear at every commencement that graduation is just a beginning.

3. Information Sharing and Teamwork Because work and organizations grow increasingly complex, teams of employees rely on each other to gather, interpret, select, and share information. As team members operate interdependently, skills in exchanging information, monitoring each member's activities, providing feedback, and backup assistance are essential. Your college or university offers opportunities in and outside the classroom for acquiring such skills, aspects of which are addressed in chapters 5 and 7.

How well does college prepare you for the new organization? Philip Gardner (1998) reviewed the literature in the area of job preparedness from the perspectives of new graduates and the employers. In one study, technical graduates (engineering, computer sciences) and liberal arts graduates evaluated their strengths and weaknesses. In general, the technical graduates rated themselves high on computer knowledge and problem solving and technical skills, but low on oral, written, and interpersonal communication skills, leadership skills, and applying learning to real-work situations. In comparison, liberal arts graduates gave themselves high marks on problem solving/independent thinking, oral, written, and interpersonal communication skills, general knowledge, and learning-to-learn skills. However, the liberal arts grads rated themselves low on the "contexts" of work such as the hands-on application of theory, computer skills, flexibility, specific content knowledge, and understanding business viewpoints, politics, and ethics. Some graduates also reported problems with self-management skills (e.g., time management) and insufficient opportunities to develop team skills.

On a positive note, studies from the employers' perspectives indicate that graduates enter the workforce with strong "domain" knowledge from their academic majors, which includes the thinking skills that contribute to that knowledge. However, employers also reported that graduates lack skills that relate to the social and contextual aspects of work. Gardner draws from previous work he performed with Garth Motschenbacher to clarify these points.

> New college workers appear to be better prepared in content- or academic-related work competencies while they show deficiencies in people-related competencies that augment their formal education. In the old hierarchical economy, where academic skills were the critical (and often sole) employment-selection criteria, young workers had the luxury of extended time in their first position to develop interpersonal, applied-reasoning, and self-management skills. Within the last decade, however, the

average tenure in one's first position has decreased by two-thirds, from approximately forty-two months in 1980 to fourteen months in 1990 (Gardner 1998, p. 73).

That many new graduates find it difficult to apply their knowledge to real-world work contexts is likely due to several factors, including unrealistic expectations, lack of sufficient work experience, failure to reach the contextual stage of knowing, and the differing learning styles in college and workplace settings. We address the issue of work experience in this chapter. Contextual knowing is examined in chapter 4: Cognitive Development During and After College: What You Should Know About Knowing. Learning styles is one of the many topics contained in chapter 6. *Read on!*

THE PARADOX OF PREPARATION

In his review of new employee transition issues, Ed Holton (1998a) reveals important insights about academic preparation. First, the core problem facing new graduates is their failure to recognize the extent to which their 17 years (or more) of education have influenced their expectations, attitudes, and behaviors regarding jobs and organizations. Second, the strategies for learning and coping developed in college may not work in the workplace.

> The paradox is that although the *knowledge* acquired in college is critical to graduates' success, the *process* of succeeding in school is very different from the process of succeeding at work. Many of the skills students developed to be successful in education processes and the behaviors for which they were rewarded are not the ones they need to be successful at work. Worse yet, the culture of education is so different that when seniors continue to have the same expectations of their employers that they did of their college and professors, they are greatly disappointed with their jobs and make costly career mistakes. Despite their best attempts to make adjustments, they cannot adjust for educational conditioning because they are not conscious of it (Holton 1998, pp. 100–101).

We believe that Ed Holton's remarks are so important that you should reread them now and periodically in the future. The major purposes of this book are to make you aware of these issues and suggest ways for you to adjust for all those years of educational conditioning.

Holton created a list of differences that new graduates perceive between college and the workplace. As you read each pair of contrasting situations in Table 2.1, ask yourself, "How difficult will it be for me to make this change between college and the workplace?"

When students in an Organizational Behavior class are shown this list, invariably, those with full-time jobs smile, nod, and concur with the accuracy of these contrasts. One student exclaimed "Now I know why I like to attend classes after a full day of work: I don't have to work at the A level *if I don't*

Table 2.1 Graduates' Perceived Differences Between College and Workplace

College	Workplace
1. Frequent and concrete feedback	Feedback infrequent and not specific
2. Some freedom to set a schedule	Less freedom or control over schedule
3. Frequent breaks and time off	Limited time off
4. Choose performance level	"A" level work expected continuously
5. Correct answers usually available	Few right answers
6. Passive participation permitted	Active participation and initiative expected
7. Independent thinking supported	Independent thinking often discouraged
8. Environment of personal support	Usually less personal support
9. Focus on personal development	Focus on getting results for organization
10. Structured courses and curriculum	Much less structure; fewer directions
11. Few changes in routine	Often constant and unexpected changes
12. Personal control over time	Responds to supervisors' directions
13. Individual effort and performance	Often, team effort and performance
14. Intellectual challenge	Organizational and people challenges
15. Acquisition of knowledge	Acquisition and application of knowledge
16. Professors	Supervisors

SOURCE: From *The Senior Year Experience* by J. N. Gardner, G Van der Veer and Associates, Chapter 7 by E. F. Holton, III (p. 102), 1998, San Francisco, CA: Jossey-Bass. This material is used by permission of John Wiley and Sons, Inc..

want to." Another student remarked that she gets feedback from her supervisor only twice a year (during performance evaluations), whereas she receives feedback from her professors several times each term. Other students point out there is so much uncertainty and constant change in their jobs that they like the rhythm, routine, and structure of college courses (*There is no syllabus in the workplace!*). Another student summed it up concisely: "In school, learning is mainly about books; at work, learning is mainly about doing."

At least one other major dimension is not reflected in Table 2.1. The daily routine for many students includes a late rising, a leisurely stroll across campus to attend class for a couple hours, a part-time job, study, and some leisure. In most full-time jobs you can expect to work for eight to ten hours consecutively, beginning at 8:00 or 9:00 A.M. five days per week and possibly some weekend days. The physical and mental adjustments required for this routine pose a serious challenge for many college grads.

Return to Holton's statement that we encouraged you to reread. When he says that the *processes* of succeeding differ from college to workplace, he is referring to your expectations, attitudes, and habits pertaining to factors such as those listed in Table 2.1. Your expectations about feedback, structure, choices, certainty, support, and the other dimensions have been shaped and sustained during your formal education from the elementary grades, through high school, and through college. It is very difficult to shake off 17 years of educational conditioning, and crossing the graduation stage, diploma in hand, does not automatically change your attitudes, expectations, or habits regarding these factors! Until the world of work is your full-time focus, you are likely to remain strongly influenced by your current educational expectations, attitudes, and habits. Some instructors, counselors, and advisors will provide valuable insights on school-to-work issues, but many cannot, especially those who have had little or no full-time work experience outside of Academia. If their professional lives have been mainly a sequence of formal educational experiences (from elementary and high school to college, to graduate school, and back to the academic world), they may not fully understand educational conditioning.

Return to the 16 dimensions in Table 2.1. Using the space below, identify three to five dimensions that will be most difficult for you to change, and those that will be easier to change.

Most difficult to adapt to: Less difficult to adapt to:

_____   _____

_____   _____

_____   _____

_____   _____

_____   _____

Talk to friends who recently entered the work force about these issues. If you have a job, analyze it in terms of the 16 dimensions; identify the organizational culture (the unwritten rules and expectations); and reflect on your interactions with coworkers and the culture. To the extent you become aware that work processes may change radically when you begin a full-time job, your "culture shock" will be lessened. So what can you do now to reduce culture shock?

WHY DON'T YOU GET A JOB!!

We'll bet that you have heard those words before, and that you currently have a job. Work helps you pay the bills, but it has other benefits that are easy to ignore. Studies relating part-time jobs to academic success generally show compatibility between the two. Many students find that outside jobs improve self-discipline and time management, enhance motivation, and contribute to good grades and satisfaction with college, *provided* there is a healthy balance of school and work. Too many students commit "academic suicide" with excessive commitments to job and school; many have major responsibilities at home. Often, hard-earned paychecks are used to repeat courses that were "bombed" because of unrealistic expectations or situations that intensify course and job demands. *Balance is essential!* What if you are among those students who, for various reasons, have not worked? What impact does lack of work experience have on your future? Read Case in Point 2.1 and find out.

CASE IN POINT 2.1 A Tale of Two Students

Shauna was a bright but shy economics major who worked hard to maintain her "B" average. She understood the importance of work experience prior to graduation and wanted a part-time job. However, she had to baby-sit for her much younger brothers and sister while her parents worked. During her senior year, she was offered a clerical job working 20 hours a week in a brokerage firm. Her parents did not want to lose their best babysitter, but they understood the importance of the job for Shauna's knowledge, self-confidence, and job prospects. She was frightened by having to *begin* her first job, as were many of us. She began with high hopes and high anxiety; there were days when she wondered if it was the correct decision. However, Shauna possessed a strong work ethic, resilience, solid interpersonal skills, and was cognizant of her limitations (a great combination of characteristics to possess in this situation). A supportive supervisor provided progressive challenges and regular, constructive feedback. During her last semester, Shauna was enrolled in a business management course that addressed many of the issues she encountered at work. By the end of the third month, Shauna had chalked-up a performance record so strong that she was offered a full-time entry-level job after graduation. In the course of a few months, Shauna's work experience was stretched from babysitting to brokerage—not exactly the stock option most students pursue.

Rob was a bright, personable, hard working, human resources major who maintained a solid "A" average throughout college and lived at home. His parents' income was high enough that Rob did not have to work, and so he didn't. During his senior year he was encouraged to apply for an internship at an area corporation. He turned it down, convinced that his "A" average, excellent study strategies, and strong academic and personal strengths were sufficient for success in his first job. About three months after graduation and several job interviews, Rob landed a position in a personnel recruitment organization, received training, and became a recruiter. The job was hard, much more difficult than he expected. Rob was willing to put in the long hours, but the fine-tuned study strategies and cognitive skills that enabled him to "ace" tests and receive glowing comments on term papers did not seem to apply in this job. Being bright gained him considerable attention during college, but being bright is not enough. Although Rob made friends easily during college, the work environment was different; sometimes he was clumsy in his social interactions with his supervisor and co-workers. Rob learned the business, experienced more than his share of "ups" and "downs" for the first couple of years, and was promoted to an assistant manager position in his third year. When he returned to college for an alumni reunion, Rob was asked what he would do differently as a student if he could repeat his last year of college. He replied quickly and firmly, "I would have taken the internship that I was offered." Because internships are such an important tool in the transition process, we will discuss them further in chapter 8.

One of the most desirable situations is to have a job related to your career plans. Robert Reardon, Janet Lenz, and Byron Folsom (1998) conducted a survey of organizational representatives who participated in a university career exposition and asked them to rate the importance of student participation in various activities. The 180 representatives who responded (33% of those sampled) rated as above average or very important "work experience that is job related" (88%), "work experience that is paid and job related" (79%), and "work experience that is not job related" (39%). To the extent you have established career goals, even if they are tentative, look for a job that connects to your goals. According to Darrell Luzzo (1996), "students who are able to obtain jobs that are related to their career interests and aspirations are more likely to experience certain vocational advantages than their peers who are not working in congruent occupations" (p. 28). Those advantages include higher levels of job satisfaction, career maturity (one's readiness to make appropriate career decisions), and the belief that career decision-making is under the individual's control (Luzzo 1996).

Work experience is still valuable even if it is not connected to your career plans. From a survey of 2000 human resources managers that yielded 1201 (60%) responses, Robert Foreman (1996) reported that 77% either consider or strongly consider an applicant's part-time employment when hiring for human resources positions. About 86% of this sample indicated that a part-time job experience could be considered *as important as grade point average* (emphasis added). If given two job applicants with equal academic qualifications, 94% would choose the applicant with part-time work experience over the person who has no work experience. Unfortunately, some students are forced to choose between a job that pays well or is nearby but unrelated to career interests and a lower-paying or distant career-related job. There may be no easy way out of this dilemma except to remember that juggling personal needs with career aspirations is a life-long challenge. Seek advice from someone you know who has faced this dilemma.

Some of you think that statistics about part-time jobs may be interesting, but you have a "dumb," mundane job that isn't going to count for anything at your next interview. Are you sure the job is that "dumb" or is your mind closed to learning from an unpleasant situation? Nearly all jobs can teach habits, skills, and attitudes transferable to other settings. For example, all jobs involve *relationships* with a supervisor and often with co-workers and customers. You are expected to communicate interactively with them, get along, and account for your actions. At minimum these relationships can teach you what to do or not to do in similar situations. Furthermore, even in a "dumb" job, you can *examine your attitudes and behaviors* toward various aspects of work. For example, do you prefer to work alone or with others? Are you punctual, reliable, and willing to work late, even when you are stressed? Do you feel comfortable accepting higher-level responsibilities, including supervising others and delegating work? Can you work in interdependent teams? Must your work be highly structured and routine or can you roll with the punches and tolerate change and ambiguity? Can you work responsibly when the tasks get dull? (Hettich, 1998)

Because such issues are inherent in most jobs, apply them to your situation even if you don't like what you are doing. Try to construct meaning from your current job in order to draw upon it in subsequent situations. Knowing what you don't want to do is useful. Sometimes part-time jobs lead to satisfying full-time employment if you have developed appropriate attitudes and work habits. For example, we recall the student who worked in the cafeteria food line her sophomore year. Her positive attitude (in spite of having to scrape food off plates), reliability, and performance led to higher responsibilities during her junior year, which led to an assistant manager position her senior year, and that concluded with an offer to manage the cafeteria at another college upon graduation. Similarly, it is difficult to predict the ways in which a job will benefit a person in later years. For example, a colleague emphasizes the important contribution of her college waitress experiences to developing the interpersonal skills required in her current position in college administration. Another colleague worked as a cafeteria worker, shampoo girl, waitress, factory worker, clerical assistant, library aide, and nurse's aide during high school and college. Surely these diverse experiences collectively contributed to her understanding of human behavior as a Ph.D. level professor of psychology.

Remember that many entry-level jobs offered to new college graduates are below their skill or interest levels. According to Eve Luppert in her *Rules for the Road* (1998), "the only way out of entry level jobs is to succeed at one" (p. 10). In such a situation, attitude may be everything! Finally, it helps to know what kind of experiences, features, and outcomes you seek in your work. Spend a few minutes reflecting on this issue by completing Case in Point 2.2.

LEARNING TO LEARN IN THE WORKPLACE: A TAXONOMY OF NEW EMPLOYEE LEARNING TASKS

Table 2.1 contrasts major differences between college and most workplaces in terms of work processes, procedures, and structures, but it does not describe the numerous tasks that new employees must learn. Holton (1998) developed a four-part taxonomy of learning tasks (based on the work of Cynthia Fisher) that serves as a conceptual model for successful entry. The taxonomy shown in Figure 2.1 consists of four "learning content" domains: individual, people, organization, and work tasks. Holton and Naquin (2001) view this model as a twelve-step program for helping new employees succeed. Each domain has three sets of tasks to be mastered by new employees. The first three domains collectively deal with organizational socialization issues such as those that Gardner indicated were absent in most graduates. The fourth domain includes tasks that are learned during job training. Organizational socialization refers to

---

CASE IN POINT 2.2   What Do You Want from Your Job?

Hellriegel, Slocum and Woodman (2004) created a scale of the 16 most mentioned characteristics that employees want from their job and presented the items in random order. Please rank the characteristics in order of both their importance to you and then in terms of satisfaction for you. Rank these characteristics 1 (most important), 2 (next most important), and so on, through 16 (least important). Use the same procedure to rank satisfaction. Then compare your answers to those of managers working in a wide variety of jobs and industries provided at the end of this exercise.

Job Characteristics	Importance Rank	Satisfaction Rank
1. Working independently	_____	_____
2. Chances for promotion	_____	_____
3. Contact with people	_____	_____
4. Flexible hours	_____	_____
5. Health insurance and other benefits	_____	_____
6. Interesting work	_____	_____
7. Work important to society	_____	_____
8. Job security	_____	_____
9. Opportunity to learn new skills	_____	_____
10. High income	_____	_____
11. Recognition from team members	_____	_____
12. Vacation time	_____	_____
13. Regular hours	_____	_____
14. Working close to home	_____	_____
15. Little job stress	_____	_____
16. A job in which I can help others	_____	_____

Answers given by managers
For job *importance,* the rank order of characteristics is 1-6; 2-14; 3-15; 4-16; 5-1; 6-2; 7-13; 8-3; 9-4; 10-11; 12-5; 13-8; 14-12; 15-10; 16-9.
For job *satisfaction,* the rank order of characteristics is 1-3; 2-14; 3-2; 4-6; 5-13; 6-4; 7-9; 8-7; 9-11; 10-12; 11-15; 12-8; 13-5; 14-1; 15-16; 16-10.

1. Which characteristics give you the greatest satisfaction? the least satisfaction? Why?
2. To what extent do situational factors (e.g., being in school, searching for a new job) influence your ranking of importance?

NOTE: From *Organizational Behavior,* 10th edition by HELLRIEGEL/SLOCUM/WOODMAN, copyright 2004. Reprinted with permission of South-Western, a division of Thomson Learning: www.thomsonrights.com. Fax 800 730-2215.

"the process through which people move from outsiders to effective, participating members of their organization . . ." (Greenberg 2002, p. 171, emphasis added). Because socialization is primarily a process, it is not directed to learning particular work tasks and procedures. Instead, it calls upon the new employee's interpersonal skills and savvy for establishing communication networks and strategies for relating to people. Ultimately, it culminates with the employee's acceptance of the organization's values and practices.

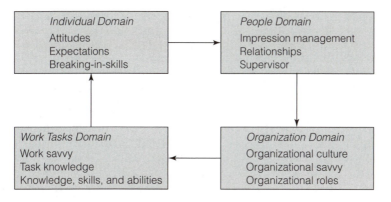

FIGURE 2.1 New Employee Development Learning Tasks

SOURCE: From *The Senior Year Experience* by J. N. Gardner, G. Van der Veer and Associates, Chapter 7 by E. F. Holton, III (p. 103), 1998, San Francisco, CA: Jossey-Bass. This material is used by permission of John Wiley and Sons, Inc..

As we sketch the twelve tasks of the four domains, apply them to one of these situations: (1) your socialization experiences as a first-year or transfer student, or (2) how you imagine you will enter the workforce as a full-time employee.

Individual Domain

The three tasks to be learned by the new graduate/employee in the *individual domain* are heavily influenced by values, beliefs, and prior experiences that you bring to the job.

- Attitude: You have heard that attitude is everything or almost everything. Attitudes can make you or break you. Your attitude includes your beliefs, judgments, and dispositions toward a person, event, or situation, whether it is a new teacher, course, or job. According to Holton and Naquin (2001), managers want to see such attitudes as adaptability, a strong work ethic, appropriate humility, open-mindedness, readiness for continual learning, and commitment. If your attitudes match those required in that situation, you are off to a good start. How do you learn the appropriate attitudes toward a new job? Begin by recalling those that were appropriate in previous work experiences (whether you possessed them or not), then listen, observe, reflect, and act.

- Expectations: Related to attitudes are the new employee's self-expectations and those developed toward the job and the organization. Employers are quick to point out that new graduates' unrealistic expectations about promotion, salary, and responsibilities contribute to bad starts. Your past work experience can be a useful guide, but not always.

- Breaking-in-skills include the employee's strong commitment to a successful entry (i.e., taking the new job seriously) and the mastery of strategies that insure this process. It is important to remember that being hired is not equivalent to being accepted, a process that is earned and takes time. Breaking-in also means to avoid criticism, conform to the new culture, and admit that there is much you need to learn (Holton and Naquin, 2001).

In conclusion, mastery of individual domain tasks is an essential stepping stone to success in the people, organization and work task domains.

If the first three tasks are not mastered, and new graduates enter the organization with inappropriate attitudes and expectations, poor impressions result. This in turn discourages people from building the strong relationships that lead to the types of organizational learning crucial to success. Relationships with supervisors are also immediately strained, potentially reducing opportunities for success-creating assignments (Holton, 1998, pp. 105).

How can you learn the three tasks in the Individual domain during college?

1. As attitudes and expectations are derived in part from your self-concept and identity, it is essential that you attempt to discover who you are, what drives you, where you want to go, and what values will take you there, *before* you take that first job. Chapter 3 explores issues of growth and identity that are important in developing realistic expectations and healthy attitudes. Chapter 6 enables you to examine your motivation from several perspectives.

2. Journalist Susan L. Taylor observed: "Thoughts are energy. And you can make your world or break your world by your thinking." Become aware of the ways in which prior educational conditioning, the media, and the beliefs of others have shaped your beliefs, attitudes, and expectations toward jobs, and then modify your views appropriately. In short, what *are* your attitudes and expectations toward full-time work, and how were they formed? Are they mature?

3. Work with a career counselor to create a plan that enables you to identify your strengths, interests, goals, and potential career fields. Develop job-search and interview skills that increase your knowledge and shape realistic expectations and attitudes. Make it your goal to begin this process long before graduation!

4. Anticipate the differences between college and corporate workplaces using Table 2.1 as a starting point. Gain meaningful work experience through jobs where you can assess the influence of these factors on your performance. Breaking-in to a new job can be one of the most exciting and valuable growth experiences in your life *if* you plan it properly.

People Domain

Holton and others believe that entering a new organization is primarily a social learning process that occurs during on-the-job-training, feedback, informal conversations, and the organization's initiation rites. (The basis for the social learning process, observational learning, is described briefly in chapter 6; chapter 7 addresses the formation of mentoring relationships and components of teamwork). These activities are organized around the three tasks of the *people domain*.

Impression Management The term *impression management* carries negative connotations because sometimes impressions are created for deceptive purposes. Yet it is normal to want to control how other people see us, and whether we like it or not others *will* form their opinions. Impression management consists of the awareness that impressions influence others' initial evaluation of a person and the employee's ability to identify and manage appropriate impressions. Verbal and nonverbal communication, dress, attitude, judgment, sensitivity to self and others, intellect, and other factors combine to create first impressions.

Relationships Relationship tasks include the graduate's awareness of the types of relationships that should be formed plus the skills to establish and maintain healthy individual and group relationships. For example, being casual with peers and teachers may have been the norm at college, but in the workplace you will need to discriminate among the occasions where differing degrees of formality or informality are the norm when interacting with peers and supervisors, and act accordingly. Chapter 7 addresses personal and work-related aspects of relationships.

Supervisor It is self-evident that good supervisor-subordinate relationships are essential, as are the skills needed to establish and manage the relationship for mutual benefit. Feedback from supervisors is essential to the progress, continuous learning, and self-development required of employees. Some supervisors will treat you with respect and assume the best of you as you try to learn and grow, whereas others will react in an opposite manner. Your challenge is to be able to work successfully with anyone, regardless of where they fit along this continuum. Research shows that supervisor-subordinate relationships are one of the major contributors to an employee's job satisfaction.

Debra Major (2000) contends that effective relationships with supervisors and co-workers are not only the heart of successful organizational socialization, but also the quality of these relationships is likely to influence future career development. If you make college an ongoing laboratory experience in the development and refining of skills in the people domain, your transition to a successful first job and a rewarding career can be relatively smooth and productive.

Organization Domain

The third component of the taxonomy consists of three related tasks.

Organizational Culture You probably learned about your college's history, traditions, and values. Similarly, a new employee will want to learn the history, traditions, and shared values of the organization, their subsequent influence on job performance, the importance of fitting in the culture, and the skills for succeeding there.

Organizational Savvy Organizational savvy is the graduate's awareness of informal factors that influence job success and the skills that use them beneficially. For example, you learned from direct experience or from friends the fine points of taking tests, registration, financial assistance, joining the best clubs, or relating to particular faculty, staff, and students. You will need savvy to survive and thrive in your new organization. After all, you will be a freshman again.

Organizational Role Your role in the organization you work for is embedded in your tasks, responsibilities, and relationships, but it may seem ambiguous, be in conflict with other roles (employee vs. parent), and it may change. Consequently, one new employee task is to learn what those roles are, especially the expectations and activities that define and limit them. Your daily interaction with supervisors, co-workers, and your tasks will shape and clarify your roles, but you must be willing to embrace ambiguity, uncertainty, and change.

Work Task Domain

When we think about *how to use* the knowledge and skills acquired during college in a new job, we tend to associate them with the *work task* domain.

Work Savvy Work savvy is your ability to apply work and life skills to a specific job. It includes such basic professional skills as communication (written, oral, interpersonal), time management, initiative, and responsibility. The extent to which these skills are mastered in college will have direct bearing on your success as a new employee. Once again, collecting that diploma does not transform you into a pro-active, responsible, effective time manager and communicator, but you may already be such a person.

Task Knowledge *Task knowledge* is the graduate's understanding of the basic tasks that comprise the job and the way to perform them successfully—what is erroneously believed to be the only major challenge of a new job.

Knowledge, Skills, and Abilities The final task is the new employee's capacity to identify and acquire the knowledge, skills, and abilities required for current and future successful performance.

Do you feel a bit overwhelmed by this taxonomy of tasks? Are you trying to figure out how you can stay in college longer (maybe go to graduate school and earn two consecutive doctorates?) to delay the daunting tasks that lie ahead? You don't have to feel anxious because earlier we advised you to acquire experience through jobs. In addition, most organizations orient (formally or informally) new employees to the people, organization, and work task domains; however the quality of the orientation programs varies. The next step is to jump in and learn from experience! You will make mistakes along the way (everyone does), but you will stumble less often because of the ideas we are sharing. It helps to remember the words of Fredrick Douglass, "If there is no struggle, there is no progress."

Consider Holton's taxonomy of new-employee learning tasks as a *road map* of situations that you will encounter in your post-college employment. If you have had significant job experience, apply it retrospectively to the taxonomy to see what ideas apply or do not apply. Take a few minutes to gain practice in applying the work-task taxonomy to a job by performing the following exercise.

Think of the most challenging paying job you have held, part-time or full-time, whether it was working in an office or slapping burgers on buns. Recall your earliest experiences with this job and apply them below to each component of the taxonomy to the best of your ability. If you have never worked, choose a job you are familiar with.

Individual Domain

Describe your attitudes, expectations, and beliefs about breaking-in the job.

_____

_____

If you could have done things differently in this domain, what would you have done?

_____

People Domain

Describe the impressions you think you made on others and your relationships with your supervisor and co-workers.

_____

_____

If you could have acted differently in this domain, what would you have done?

_____

Organization Domain

Describe the organizational culture, your savvy with the informal aspects of the organization, and what you learned about your role there.

_____

_____

What could you have done differently to become aware of the culture, your role, and the informal dimensions of the workplace?

_____

Work Task Domain

Describe the savvy, knowledge, skills, and abilities needed for this job.

_____

_____

If you had this job again, what aspects of this domain would you have done differently?

_____

CASE IN POINT 2.3   The Case for Confronting Conflict

Conflict occurs when you believe that others are interfering with your interests or goals (Hellriegel, Slocum, and Woodman 2004). You have confronted your share of conflicts; some may have led to personal growth. In all organizations, including your college or university, individuals may encounter four levels of conflict: (1) *inter-group* (e.g., between student groups, faculty and administration, or departments within your company), (2) *intra-group* (e.g., within your social organization, work group, or circle of friends), (3) *inter-personal* (e.g., between roommates, student and teacher, or coworkers), and (4) *intra-personal* (e.g., conflicts involving your goals, feelings, or behaviors).

Inter-group, intra-group, and inter-personal conflicts are often based on the ways that others use or misuse power. There are five types of power that people around you can exert, sometimes simultaneously. *Reward* power is the ability to provide rewards such as praise and privileges, while *coercive* power is the ability to punish. *Legitimate* power is a person's ability to influence your behavior because of his or her formal or appointed position in the organization, such as supervisor, resident assistant, instructor, or parent. Some individuals have *expert* power because of particular skills or knowledge they possess (e.g., as a computer technician, financial assistance staff member, or Archeology professor). If a person is highly respected or admired for particular qualities or experiences (e.g., the beloved student activities director, award-winning teacher, successful executive, war veteran), he or she possesses *referent* power.

Often you experience conflict when others exercise their power: The financial assistance staffer refuses to increase your aid; your supervisor demands you work late the evening before an exam; an instructor refuses to give you a make-up test; or a "significant other" tells you to move out. Such situations can create profound conflict and stress. Researchers have identified different styles individuals use to deal with interpersonal conflict; the model presented here reflects five combinations of a person's level of cooperativeness and assertiveness (Hellriegel, Slocum, and Woodman 2004). Individuals who use the *avoiding style* in the face of conflict may act passively and uncooperatively, ignore disagreements, remain neutral, and believe the conflict will resolve itself. Avoidance may be appropriate when the conflict involves minor issues, persons lack information or insufficient power to effect change, or when others can resolve the issue more effectively. However, avoiding conflicts often frustrates other people, prevents everyone involved from reaching goals, and can generate negative evaluations from others.

Individuals using the *forcing style* act assertively but uncooperatively in a win-lose approach to solving problems. Coercive power is used to achieve goals by forcing one's will on others in a way that ignores their input and reduces their work motivation. Resolving conflict through

---

Holton's taxonomy is an excellent *outline* of the steps new employees must follow and the tasks to be mastered. They involve highly complex configurations of behaviors, attitudes, and skills that often occur subtly in ordinary situations. For example, how should the new employee deal with office politics, professional attire, making mistakes, sexually intense situations, participating in a meeting, or even having a business lunch with a

CASE IN POINT 2.3　Continued

force may be necessary when an unpopular decision must be made for long-term benefits, during an emergency, or to protect a person from others' coercions, but is not a style favored by most people.

In contrast, an *accommodating style* reflects a cooperative but unassertive approach to conflict. Individuals sacrifice personal concerns and goals for the good of others to reduce disagreement and bring harmony. Accommodation may be necessary to deal with short-term problems, volatile situations, and certain "difficult" persons. However, although accommodating individuals are generally liked, consistent selfless behavior may be judged as weakness by others.

In the *collaborating style* persons act cooperatively and assertively in a win-win approach that emphasizes everyone's strengths. People who collaborate are trustful, accept conflict as a natural, even helpful, means of reaching goals, and realize this style generates stronger satisfaction and commitment to the solution than other approaches. Collaboration usually requires more time and involvement, but it is appropriate when power is approximately equal, cooperation is desirable, and benefits accrue to all. Collaboration is associated with successful individuals, positive feelings in self and others, and high performing organizations.

The fifth and final style, *compromising,* reflects levels of cooperation and assertiveness midway between the highs and lows of the other approaches in a give-and-take

process to solving problems. Generally, people who can compromise are favorably evaluated because this style helps maintain good relations, demonstrates willingness for some sacrifice, and is a practical strategy (Hellriegel, Slocum, and Woodman 2004).

Knowing about conflict, power, and styles of conflict-management is a good first step for strengthening your ability to manage conflict in your environment. Spend a few minutes to apply these concepts to your situation by responding to these items.

1. Where do you see examples of inter-group and intra-group conflict in your college or job settings?
2. List a few interpersonal conflicts you experience and identify the specific style you use to resolve each. Based on information presented above, to what extent are your styles appropriate to each situation?
3. What significant intrapersonal conflicts are you currently experiencing? To what extent do they spill over to your coursework, job, or relationships?

Campus counseling or wellness centers are often the best source of information for learning strategies that enable you to manage conflicts. Finally, the patterns you have developed for resolving conflict are likely to follow you into the workplace and in your relationships. Are you satisfied with the styles you use? Using your remaining academic terms to identify and strengthen your skills in this critically important aspect of relationships.

supervisor? For example, we know of a student whose application for a job was rejected in part because he ordered an alcoholic beverage at lunch when his interviewers, who ordered first, chose not to. Although situations like this are best approached with common sense, much is learned from experience, co-workers, mentors, and sources such as Arndt and Ricchini's compact *Backpack to Briefcase: Steps to a Successful Career.* Case in Point 2.3

is a primer for understanding one very important dimension each of us encounters daily and especially as new employees, namely conflict.

WHAT ELSE CAN I DO?

In subsequent chapters, we will address some of the topics below in greater detail.

1. Take courses that focus directly on specific organizational aspects of the workplace such as management, communication and group skills, organizational behavior, the sociology of organizations, career planning, leadership, human resources, and internships. View group projects, class debates, and problem-solving groups as skill-building opportunities not drudgery.

2. Take advantage of workshops or seminars that focus on self-development, leadership, conflict management, team building, interpersonal communication, time management, stress management, and similar generic professional skills.

3. Join clubs, sports, and campus organizations where collaboration, teamwork, conflict, communication, and leadership are constructive tools for accomplishing the organization's objectives. Focus on the processes used to reach the outcomes, not just the outcomes.

4. Begin to collect evidence of your achievements, including papers, projects, awards, and performance evaluations. In chapter 5, we discuss the importance of organizing a portfolio.

5. Do not expect that we will give you all the answers! We cannot because we do not know them. Besides, there's no substitute for experience and your ability to thoughtfully reflect on your experiences.

6. Do not be surprised if the day after your graduating class is told how smart they are, you have to demonstrate your computer skills to a potential employer.

CONCLUDING COMMENTS

We may have alarmed you with remarks about the changing nature of work, the impact of prior educational conditioning, and the new employee learning tasks. If we did, we are pleased that you encountered these issues now, at a time when you can explore them and act on our suggestions, rather than in a state of trauma or depression during your first month in a new job. When we ask recent graduates to describe their first year out of college, it's not unusual to hear, "It was a slap in the face!" or "It was a rude awakening to the real world!" or "I never expected it to be this way!" These are actual responses! We do not want you to repeat such remarks.

JOURNAL STARTERS

1. Think about the jobs (paid or volunteer) you liked most and least. For each job, identify the specific aspects you liked most and least, and describe how they affected you. How can you connect these most- and least-liked factors to topics discussed in this chapter?

2. Are you a transfer student who found the adjustment to your new institution challenging? If so, apply the four new work-task domains to your transfer experience. Do not expect a perfect fit between the taxonomy and your transfer, but you should find many similarities in the new tasks you had to learn.

3. What were the two most significant insights you gained from reading this chapter? What issues concern you most?

FYI

www.LifeAfterGraduation.com—more information about the Arndt and Ricchini book below
www.jobweb.com—information about jobs and job-related issues

REFERENCES

Arndt, T., and Ricchini, J. (2003). *Backpack to briefcase: Steps to a successful career.* Alexandria, VA: Life After Graduation, LLC.

Bridges, W. (1994). *Job shift: How to prosper in a workplace without jobs.* Reading, MA: Addison-Wesley.

Foreman, R. (1996). UPS study relates student employment to job-hunting success after graduation. In Kincaid, R (Ed.) *Student employment: Linking college and the workplace.* Columbia, SC: National Resource Center for the Freshman Year Experience & Students in Transition.

Gardner, P. D. (1998). Are college seniors prepared to work? In J. N. Gardner, G. Van der Veer & Associates, *The senior year experience: Facilitating integration, reflection, closure and transition* (pp. 60–80). San Francisco, CA: Jossey-Bass.

Greenberg, J. (2002). *Managing Behavior in Organizations* (3rd ed.). Upper Saddle River, NJ: Prentice Hall.

Hellriegel, D., Slocum, Jr., J. W., and Woodman, R.W. (2004). *Organizational behavior* (10th ed.). Thompson/Southwestern.

Hettich, P. (1998). Learning Skills for College and Career. Pacific Grove, CA: Brooks/Cole.

Holton, E. F. III (1998a). Preparing students for life beyond the classroom. In J. N. Gardner, G. Van der Veer & Associates, *The senior year experience: Facilitating integration, reflection, closure and transition* (pp. 95–115). San Francisco, CA: Jossey-Bass.

Holton, E. F., and Naquin, S. (2001). *So you're new again.* San Francisco, CA: Berrett-Kohler Publishers, Inc.

Lieber, R. (1999, June). First jobs aren't child's play. *Fast Company.* pp. 154–160, 164, 166, 170–171.

Luppert, E. (1998). *Rules for the road: Surviving your first job out of school.* New York, NY: The Berkley Publishing Group.

Luzzo, D. A. (1996). Career decision-making benefits of college student employment. In Kincaid, R. (Ed.). *Student employment: Linking college and the workplace.* Columbia, SC: National Resource Center for The Freshman Year Experience & Students in Transition.

Major, D. A. (2000). Effective newcomer socialization into high-performance organizational cultures. In N. M. Ashkanasy, C. P. M. Wilderom, and M. F. Peterson (Editors). *Handbook of organizational culture and climate.* Thousand Oaks, CA: Sage Publications.

Reardon, R., Lenz, J. G., and Folsom, B. (1998). Employer ratings of student participation in non-classroom-based activities: Findings from a campus survey. Journal of Career Planning and Employment, 58(4), 36–39.

Thau, R. D., and Heflin, J. S. (1997). *Get it together by 30: And be set for the rest of your life.* New York, NY: American Management Association.

3

Coming of Age: Young Adult Development

It doesn't interest me where or what or with whom you have studied.
I want to know what sustains you, from the inside, when all else falls away.
I want to know if you can be alone with yourself and if you truly like the
company you keep in the empty moments.

ORIAH MOUNTAIN DREAMER*

It was the end of Christmas break, and Andrew was returning to his junior
year of college. Chatting with his mother while driving along, he said,
"Wow, it's already the second semester of my junior year. College is almost
over." Asked if he was excited about the prospect of finishing school, he
responded, "Not really . . . the working full-time thing . . . living on my
own and paying my own bills . . . it's just that, when I think of the word
'adult,' my own picture does not come to mind." Andrew, usually laid-back
and easy-going, did not worry about much. His mother was surprised to find
not a hint of humor in his words, his tone, or his expression.

Andrew had adjusted well to college, as he had to most things in his life. He
had good grades and had successfully completed an internship in the county
court system. He was active in his fraternity and enjoyed a full complement of
relationships. His anxiety about his future seemed out of sync with the reality of
his life. Yet his older brother, Matthew, who had graduated from the same university a year earlier, was indeed finding adjustment to adulthood a challenge.

Matthew had excellent grades throughout college and was a gifted communicator. Many of his professors had encouraged him to publish his papers.

* From *The Invitation*, by Oriah Mountain Dreamer. Copyright 1999 by Oriah Mountain Dreamer. Reprinted by permission of Harper Collins Publishers, Inc.

He brought an intensity, a powerful intellect, and a rapier wit to his work and his relationships. But after graduation, Matthew had simply stalled out. He had spent the year avoiding a serious job search. His part-time job barely paid his bills. His relationships were suffering; he was suffering; yet he didn't seem able to take any positive steps.

GROWING PAINS

At the time, we did not have a name for what had happened to Matthew and would, perhaps, happen to Andrew as well. However, we had seen it occur many times during our years in higher education. Something befalls many students—good, bright, motivated students—as college draws to a close. While we recognized the pattern, it didn't seem to fit particularly well with the developmental theories that are used as indicators when working with young adults.

Theories of human development can be wonderful guides—maps, if you will—of the terrain of life. These theories provide a general framework of the challenges attached to each life stage and the expected personal growth that rewards you when you rise to meet these challenges. While it is useful to understand developmental theory, it is imperative to recognize that the path to adulthood is not a straight one. Developmental theories offer clarity; yet, the most salient component of young adulthood is confusion! How is this possible? Are the theories false? Or do the demands of the world require something more of young adults today than of college graduates of previous generations? Chickering and Reisser (1993) believe something quite different is required of individuals in the twenty-first century.

> In earlier eras, the principal task of education was "socialization," and the problem of individuals was to learn the attitudes, actions, and skills necessary for a satisfying and productive fit with "society." The symphony had a clearly stated theme and rhythm. The types and positions of the instruments were settled. To contribute, one had merely to choose a standard instrument, learn to play it, practice the part. In the global society of the twenty-first century, where change is the only certainty, not socialization but identity formation becomes the central and continuing task of education. With a firm sense of self as artist—as performer, composer, improviser, and conductor—tomorrow's graduates will not be bound to a single instrument. Regardless of the roles they assume or the demands of the performance, they will know how to bring forth their best talents and contribute to the greater whole. And if need be, they can go out and form their own ensemble (p. 208).

It is not that key developmental theorists have ignored young adulthood; it is that their explanations do not seem to capture the full experience of this passage. Young adulthood is characterized by the struggle to carve out and embrace an identity, a place in the world, and a way to make meaning and find purpose. All of this is happening in the context of leaving college. Matt, a graduate student, writes eloquently of this dilemma:

> Somehow as a student moves from freshman to senior year, things often do not seem as crystal clear anymore. As students approach senior year, they become increasingly filled with doubt about their future . . . Family parties are met with dread as the inevitable question on everyone's lips is, "So what are your plans for next year?" That question rings as an accusation . . . Many students are graduating and still do not know what they want to be when they "grow up." For four years, or more, these students have been in an incubated semi-adult world. They have been able to make their own decisions about what classes to take, who their friends are, who they are within the safe confines of a university campus . . . Suddenly, they are thrust into the "real world." More often than not this is a reality for which they are painfully under-prepared.

If this predicament feels uncomfortably familiar and you are between the ages of eighteen and thirty, then welcome to young adulthood.

THEORETICALLY SPEAKING

It seems useful, at this point, to investigate some key developmental theories and discover what exactly they do tell us about young adulthood.

Erik Erikson's Eight Stages
of Psychosocial Development

Erikson believed that development took place across the lifespan. In fact, he was the first to recognize stages of development beyond childhood. Erikson's theory outlines eight sequential stages of development (see Table 3.1). Each new stage occurs when internal biological and psychological changes interact with environmental demands, producing a developmental task or challenge. "Resolution of developmental tasks is influenced by how successful the individual is in developing appropriate coping skills. An optimal balance of challenge and support in the environment facilitates such development" (Evans, Forney, Guido-DiBrito 1998, p. 33).

The first four stages of Erikson's theory span the period from infancy to early adolescence. If developmental challenges have been met, individuals emerge from stage four with the groundwork laid for identity formation. Clarifying and embracing identity, then, is the goal of stage five and the work of adolescence—work that Erikson sees as almost complete by the time an individual is entering college. Stage six, the focus of young adulthood, requires the capacity to develop and maintain intimate relationships. The last two stages demand that individuals find a way to mentor the next generations and find acceptance of and satisfaction in the lives they have lived.

Table 3.1 Erik Erikson's Eight Stages of Psychosocial Development

Stage	Ages	Basic Conflict	Summary
1. Oral-Sensory	Birth–18 mo.	Trust v. Mistrust	Infant must form a first loving, trusting relationship with caregiver or develop a sense of mistrust.
2. Muscular-Anal	18–36 mo.	Autonomy v. Shame/Doubt	Child's energies directed toward development of physical skills. Child learns control but may feel shame and doubt if handled poorly.
3. Locomotor	3–6 yrs.	Initiative v. Guilt	Child becomes more assertive and takes more initiative, but acting with too much force may lead to guilt feelings.
4. Latency	6–12 yrs.	Industry v. Inferiority	Child must deal with demands to learn new skills (especially in school) or risk feeling incompetent.
5. Adolescence	12–18 yrs.	Identity v. Role Confusion	Teenager must achieve a sense of identity in occupation, sex roles, politics, and religion.
6. Young Adulthood	19–40 yrs.	Intimacy v. Isolation	Young adult must develop intimate relationships or feel isolated.
7. Middle Adulthood	40–65 yrs.	Generativity v. Stagnation	Adult must find a way to satisfy and support the next generation.
8. Maturity	65–death	Ego Integrity v. Despair	Acceptance of the self and the life one has lived brings a sense of fulfillment.

SOURCE: Adapted from Cramer, Flynn and LaFave, 1997, Erik Erikson's 8 Stages of Psychosocial Development, http://facultyweb.cortland.edu/~ANDERSMD/ERIK/welcome.HTML

Stages five and six are of greatest interest to young adult development; therefore, a closer look is warranted. In stage five, in order to answer the "who am I" question, adolescents are required to view themselves as separate from their parents, which in turn enables them to make deliberate decisions and choices. In other words, it is a conscious search for self that all adolescents must make. Life choices—especially those about vocation and sexuality—are particularly important in bringing the search to a positive conclusion. According to Erikson, resolution of the developmental tasks presented in stage five should be evident by age 18. This is certainly not the experience of most 18-year-olds. While many college freshman enter college believing they have made their career and sexual choices, it is the very rare student who does not question these choices during his/her college experience. In fact, it is much more typical for students to unmake and remake these choices several times during college. Sharon Daloz Parks, in 2001 speech at Loyola University Chicago, suggested that the true intent of higher education is to "mess up" students' ways of making meaning.

Stage six and the establishment of intimacy occupies most of early adulthood, according to Erikson. Intimacy is not to be confused with sex. Erikson's definition of intimacy is the ability to relate to and commit to another on a deeply personal level. The two stages in combination ask that each individual can be wholly committed to another human being while maintaining a strong and clear sense of self. In stage six, Erikson extends young adulthood to 40 years of age, but confines the developmental struggle to relationship issues. College students do, of course, wrestle with relationships. It is, however, only one of the many important life issues they confront during and after their college years.

James Marcia and Identity Status

James Marcia, a developmental theorist who began studying college students in the 1960s, broke Erikson's stage five into four identity statuses: (1) identity achievement, (2) moratorium, (3) foreclosure, and (4) identity diffusion (McAdams 2001). Each status depicts a particular developmental position held by an individual regarding his/her willingness to explore and to commit to areas of life that Erikson believed were central to identity. These areas are occupation (what work will I do) and values (what do I believe), especially regarding religion and politics.

Young adults who have actively questioned their career and values decisions and have made commitments to occupation and ideology that are critically thought through and well articulated have reached identity achievement, the most developmentally advanced of Marcia's four statuses. Identity achievers are typically self-reliant, have internalized their goals, and make decisions in an autonomous and principled way.

Young adults in moratorium status have explored the questions of work and values, but have not made decisions yet. While a lack of commitment can and often does lead to an identity crisis, Marcia viewed moratoriums as mature. They may not know where to find the answers, but they are asking the necessary questions and searching for responses that "fit" them. Moratoriums, like identity achievers, have a richer and more individualized sense of self.

Young adults who have failed to meet the challenges of Erikson's stage five occupy the foreclosure and identity diffusion statuses. Foreclosures have committed to career and values without the benefit of exploration. Their childhood commitments remain unquestioned; they "choose" to believe and do exactly what important authority figures in their lives have required of them. Foreclosures have conventional values, rigid standards of right and wrong, and a willingness to submit to a strong, external authority. Identity diffusions, on the other hand, have not searched for answers to life's big questions or made any commitments. With little from the past to draw upon and no future to plan for, they seem to be "born new every day." Because there is not much for identity diffusions to hold on to, they are best characterized by social isolation and withdrawal.

Marcia discovered that today's moratoriums are usually tomorrow's identity achievers; however, foreclosures and identity diffusions do not typically move up the developmental ladder as young adults. While foreclosures may have avoided an early identity crisis, they are ripe for one at a later point. Often it is a "mid-life crisis" that catapults foreclosures into seeking their own answers to the big identity questions. Identity diffusions may go through their entire lives without the identity anchors that offer them a true sense of self.

Higher Education and Foreclosed Identity Many students enter college with a declared major and a career to which they aspire. Most of the students in this "decided" group made these enormous, life-directing choices without the benefit of factual, or even anecdotal, information. These "I declared my major and I know what I'm doing when I graduate" students have chosen their academic direction and life's work based on parental expectations, family career history, the careers of their role models, a valued teacher's occupational suggestion, or even their favorite television shows. While it comes as no surprise that many first-year students begin their collegiate lives with foreclosed career identities, the fact that institutions of higher education seem to prefer students this way is not only surprising, it is alarming.

Admissions counselors for colleges and universities are trained to ask prospective students, almost immediately, about major and/or career interests. If the student says that he/she is considering broadcasting, the admissions representative can now focus on providing information about the school of communications and requirements for media majors. As the admissions process continues, the student will receive a letter from the dean of the communications school, a call from the chair of the media department, an e-mail from a student who is a media major doing an internship for CNN. At registration (usually the summer before freshman year), the student will select courses with an academic advisor from the school of communications. Presto! A broadcaster is born!

Accepting media as a major is easy for the student. With a career decision made, he/she can move on to the more important aspects of college, like making friends and finding decent food on campus. Parents are pleased that their child has a direction and their money won't be wasted while their freshman figures things out. The school is pleased because it is easier to advise and plan for "declared" students. It is rare for the student to meet someone who asks, "why broadcasting?" or "what other things have you thought about?" The entire system appears to unwittingly conspire to keep the student's identity foreclosed. Life in general, and higher education in particular, seems to favor people who know what they want.

For many foreclosures, the reality of a major or career choice makes itself known early in their academic lives. The media major, who is not a strong writer, discovers that exceptional writing skills are critical to success in the major and the field, that a CNN internship is the exception rather than the rule, or that the typical location of a first job in broadcasting is three miles left of the end of the universe. Some foreclosures get through school and into their first jobs, however, before they realize that asking "why" and "what else" would have been helpful. Students must decide to be seekers with or without the help of their colleges and universities. (Chapter 8 outlines processes and strategies to assist you in your quest to know yourself, the world of work, and your calling.) Moving to a position of "not knowing" (moratorium identity status) is uncomfortable but essential to career and life satisfaction.

Chickering and Reisser: The Seven Vectors

Arthur Chickering (1969, 1993) offered the world of higher education a paradigm for the psychosocial development of college students. His seven vectors resonated with the experience of college and university educators and became a tool that guided the design and implementation of university courses, programs, and services.

Unlike Erikson, the vectors were not a stage model, but a mapping device. A student's development could proceed at different rates along several vectors simultaneously. The seven vectors, however, are sequenced. This is based on the concept that all college students encounter the issues presented in the first four vectors at the beginning of their college experience. Successful movement along the first four provides a foundation from which to work on the remaining three vectors.

Chickering was joined by Linda Reisser (1993) and revised the seven vectors to be more inclusive of the experiences of nontraditional students, women, and members of minority groups. An overview of the seven vectors is provided in Table 3.2.

Chickering and Reisser's seven vectors (1993) are founded on "an optimistic view of human development, assuming that a nurturing, challenging college environment will help students grow in status and substance"(p. 40). They intentionally kept their model broad, believing that "college students live out recurring themes: gaining competence and self-awareness, learning control and flexibility, balancing intimacy with freedom, finding one's voice or vocation, refining beliefs, and making commitments" (p. 35). They also assume that as students make their journey along the vectors, they will "grow in versatility, strength, and ability to adapt when unexpected barriers or pitfalls appear" (p. 35).

Perhaps, these positive assumptions are not only the greatest strength of the seven vectors but also the greatest weakness. Chickering and Reisser seem to suggest that if you make good and constructive choices throughout your college journey, you will have the tools you need to carry you through difficult life passages and will find satisfaction and fulfillment. While this is probably the case, it is also a big-picture, there's-a-reason-for-everything, future-oriented perspective. This point of view is often very difficult for

Table 3.2 Chickering and Reisser: The Seven Vectors

	From . . .	*To . . .*
Vector 1		
Developing Competence	Low level of intellectual, physical, and interpersonal confidence	High level of competence
	Lack of confidence in abilities	Strong sense of competence
Vector 2		
Managing Emotions	Little control over disruptive emotions (fear, anxiety, anger and aggression, guilt, shame, dysfunctional sexual/romantic attraction)	Flexible control and appropriate expression of emotions
	Little awareness of feelings	Increasing awareness and acceptance of emotions
	Inability to integrate feelings with actions	Able to integrate emotion with responsible action
Vector 3		
Moving Through Autonomy Toward Interdependence	Emotional dependence	Freedom from continual need for reassurance
	Poor self-direction or ability to problem solve; little freedom or confidence to be mobile	Instrumental independence (inner direction, persistence, and mobility)
	Independence	Acceptance of interdependence
Vector 4		
Developing Mature Interpersonal Relationships	Lacks awareness or intolerance of differences	Tolerance and appreciation of differences
	Non-existent, short-term, or unhealthy intimate relationships	Capacity for intimacy that is enduring and nurturing
Vector 5		
Establishing Identity	Discomfort with body and appearance	Comfort with body and appearance
	Discomfort with gender and sexual orientation	Comfort with gender and sexual orientation
	Lacks clarity about heritage, social/cultural roots of identity	Sense of self in a social, historical, and cultural context
	Confusion about "who I am" and experimentation with roles and lifestyle	Clarification of self-concept through roles and lifestyle
	Lacks clarity about others' evaluation	Sense of self in response to feedback from valued others
	Dissatisfaction with self	Self-acceptance and self-esteem
	Unstable, fragmented personality	Personal stability and integration

Table 3.2 Continued

	From . . .	To . . .
Vector 6		
Developing Purpose	Unclear vocational goals	Clear vocational goals
	Shallow, scattered personal interests	Sustained, focused, rewarding activities
	Few meaningful interpersonal commitments	Strong interpersonal and family commitments
Vector 7		
Developing Integrity	Dualistic thinking and rigid beliefs	Humanizing values
	Unclear or untested personal values and beliefs	Personalizing (clarifying and affirming) values while respecting others' beliefs
	Self-interest	Social responsibility
	Discrepancies between values and actions	Congruence and authenticity

SOURCE: Adapted from Chickering and Reisser, Education and Identity, 2nd ed. p. 38-39. Copyright 1993. This material used by permission of Wiley and Sons, Inc.

college students to embrace because their focus is typically riveted on the demands of the here-and-now. The seven vectors give no voice to the immediate, to the impact of setbacks and crises, or to just plain changing your mind. While they hesitate to attach timing to movement through the vectors, the ideal suggests that most of this growth is accomplished while attaining an undergraduate degree. A considerable amount of the work is, in fact, achieved while in college; however, the fruit of that labor is not always apparent at graduation.

Most college graduates have certainly made some headway along vector six, developing purpose, and vector seven, developing integrity. But the developmental work of these two areas seems to intensify in the years after college. Developing purpose (vector six) focuses on vocational and relational commitments. In general, the early-to-mid-twenties finds individuals coming face-to-face with the fact that the reality of a particular career does not match their dreams and visions. Consequently, changing jobs is a given, and changing careers is typical. For the first time in the lives of many young adults, relationships also become a challenge. The college experience usually offers a built-in community. College graduation marks the end of easy access to peers and activities. Young adults find that they must work at creating and maintaining relationships; they must now actively build their own communities or face feeling alone and isolated.

Vector seven, developing integrity, is tricky in that college life facilitates access to socially responsible, belief-based activities in a way that the subsequent years do not. While in school, social justice and volunteer options abound.

Many universities offer course credit for community service. Speakers of all backgrounds and social perspectives are brought to campus. Students have a banquet of choices at their fingertips and live in an environment that encourages and rewards their participation. After graduation the applause dies down. A boss doesn't give extra points for working in a soup kitchen instead of staying at the office to meet a deadline. Attending a lecture means searching it out and paying for admission. Participating in a Habitat for Humanity project over spring break becomes impossible because there is no spring break; now it means giving up one of the two precious weeks a year that is allotted as vacation time.

Traveling along the Vectors Chickering and Reisser's seven vectors of psychosocial development are listed below. Map your progress along each of the vectors, using a scale of "1"=*have not accomplished any of developmental tasks of the vector* to "5"=*have accomplished all of the developmental tasks of the vector.*

Vector 1—Developing Competence
Believes in abilities; highly competent intellectual, physical and interpersonal skills
Rating for Vector 1: _____

Explanation of Rating: _____

Vector 2—Managing Emotions
Able to appropriately control and express feelings; aware and accepting of emotions; feelings and behaviors are congruent
Rating for Vector 2: _____

Explanation of Rating: _____

Vector 3—Moving through Autonomy toward Interdependence
Internally-motivated; strong problem solver; finds on-going reassurance unnecessary; accepts interdependence
Rating for Vector 3: _____

Explanation of Rating: _____

Vector 4—Developing Mature Interpersonal Relationships
Appreciates differences; participates in committed, emotionally intimate relationships
Rating for Vector 4: _____

Explanation of Rating: _____

Vector 5—Establishing Identity
Understands personal identity within cultural, historical, social, role, and lifestyle contexts; values physical, gender, and sexual aspects of self; values others' feedback and integrates it as appropriate; is satisfied and appreciates self

Rating for Vector 5: _____

Explanation of Rating: _____

Vector 6—Developing Purpose
Vocational goals and personal interests clear and rewarding; maintains strong interpersonal and family commitments
Rating for Vector 6: _____

Explanation of Rating: _____

Vector 7—Developing Integrity
Clarifies and affirms personal values; respects others' values; actions are socially responsible and personally authentic
Rating for Vector 7: _____

Explanation of Rating: _____

So What's Missing?

Young adults are often caught between the person they would like to be and the person they believe they need to be in order to be "successful." The battle to be an authentic human being is far from over at college graduation; it is, in fact, just beginning.

Although there is some overlap among Erikson's stages, it is generally believed that his identity stage ends where most college students begin and that his intimacy stage is limited in scope but extended in the amount of time given to achieve it. Marcia gives us a clearer identity picture but is fuzzy on movement from one status to another. Chickering and Reisser are more specific about the passages of young adulthood but seem to require a trip through the vectors in four to five years. While these theories give us a useful way to think about developmental issues, they seem to miss the way in which most people experience their own growth and maturation. The following are true stories that shine a bright light on the difference between theory and practice.

THE MESSY, MURKY METAMORPHOSIS
OF YOUNG ADULTHOOD

Human growth and development is predicated upon change. Change is, by its very nature, a nebulous and untidy process. It calls upon us to take risks, to jump without being able to see a net, to believe in our own power and light. Therefore, people don't come to change willingly; in fact, it is usually accomplished with a great deal of kicking and screaming. In general, change occurs because the pain of staying the same is too great. Transformation is the outcome of the always difficult, often frustrating, and sometimes frightening work of change.

As you read the following stories, compare and contrast the demands of each person's journey through young adulthood and the winding roads that each one takes through the process of transformation. Later in the chapter you will discover that the struggles these young adults faced are not only common, but perhaps necessary to the "growing up" process.

Karen

In the winter of her senior year, Karen found herself on her way to medical school. She had double-majored in English and biology, and she had terrific GPA and MCAT scores. She had volunteered in a hospital emergency room and a home for the elderly. Her family was proud of her plan to be a doctor. In fact, her parents had been focused on this goal for as long as she could remember. So why was Karen deferring entry to medical school for a year?

Karen was one of those multi-talented individuals who always won first prize for the most creative Halloween costume, had a column in the school paper, and could name all the bones in the human body. She was an academic golden girl who had always been on the fast track. This track had come to an abrupt end in the second semester of her senior year. She had a difficult time explaining why she was so unhappy that she had not been attending classes, completing assignments, or leaving her apartment very often. She couldn't seem to move forward or in any other direction for that matter. She was hiding—from her teachers, from her family, and from herself.

Over the next few weeks, Karen was able to focus on her schoolwork enough to complete all assignments and graduate in May, however, she had absolutely no career plan. She finally acknowledged that she hated the sight of blood, didn't much like sick people, and had never really wanted to be a doctor. She was afraid of disappointing her family and her teachers; but she was more afraid to take on a career that would make her miserable. Karen was a 21-year-old college graduate who had never given a moment's thought to a career other than medicine. She was a woman without a future as far as she was concerned.

During the next several months, Karen took some short-term work to pay the bills and gave herself permission to explore new career paths. She gathered information on design careers that would take advantage of her artistic talents, library careers that would speak to her writing ability and her love of literature, and computer science careers that would utilize her strengths in math and science. She took an art class and a computer science class. She took a full-time job in a library. She went to bartenders' school. Two years after graduation, she made the decision to pursue a master's degree in computer science. Three years after graduation, she got a part-time position in the information technology division of a university and assisted in the design and maintenance of their web site. Five years after her undergraduate experience, she had completed her master of computer science degree and was the director of the department that managed the web site for a prestigious midwestern university.

Jim

Jim had been actively involved in the co-curricular life of the university and had done well academically. He graduated with a degree in psychology and a sense that he wanted to do something important. He moved into his parents' home after graduation, a temporary measure until he found work. Six months after graduation, he was still living with his parents and no closer to a full-time job. Jim would make appearances in the career center and chat about his progress in finding a job, however, he did not share the difficulty that he was having.

Jim's frustration with himself and the entire process of establishing himself as an independent person was palpable. He was completely overwhelmed by all that needed to be accomplished and had no idea how to proceed. He believed that, since he had wasted so much time, every move had to be the absolute right one—there was no room for error anymore. Since he could never be sure that the next thing he chose would be "the right" thing, he found himself unable to make any choices at all.

By the following summer (one full year after graduation), Jim had taken a position working with physically and mentally disabled children. He found the work difficult but rewarding. His success there gave him the energy to explore other options. He applied for and was accepted into AmeriCorps. Eighteen months after his graduation, he began his AmeriCorps training. His year of service in AmeriCorps took place on the east coast. During that time, he worked on several community service projects including an AIDS education program and in-class tutoring for children from an inner-city school. AmeriCorps also provided him with a community of peers, an environment in which he blossomed.

Jim's return to the midwest found him better prepared to make vocational commitments, and he took a tutoring position at a community college. His tutees are adults for whom English is not their first language. He had to search once again for a sense of community, and he still fights against the isolation that being a single, working adult in the city can breed.

Ana

Ana is typical of thousands of second semester seniors. Throughout her college career Ana's goal was to become a clinical psychologist. Last semester Ana completed an internship working with children who had a history of abuse and neglect. Ana did not enjoy the work. She was panicked and angry with herself. Her panic came from suddenly having no clear career goal and feeling very out-of-step, given she was graduating in four months. Her anger was a function of her belief that she was letting her entire family down.

What was Ana's vision of clinical psychology and what had happened in the course of her internship that lead her to the conclusion that it was not the field for her? When Ana thought of clinical psychology, she thought of a room where things were clean and orderly. Her job was to sit in a big chair and offer her insight to people who sought it. She would help them, and they would be grateful to her. Her internship exposed her to the suffering of others—suffering that she couldn't prevent or find a way to heal. It was anything but sterile and, while the children and their families were feeling many things, gratitude was usually not at the top of the list.

As Ana talked about her parents, it became clear that they were supportive of her need to change. They wanted her to do something that made her happy; if clinical psychology wasn't it, then so be it. Ana was holding on to all the sacrifices that her parents had made, however, feeling that she must justify those sacrifices by doing something wonderful and doing it immediately upon graduation. In her own mind, making them proud of her left no room for confusion or doubt.

Ana has a long road in front of her. She needs to achieve some relationship clarity to separate out her parents' issues from her own. She also needs to further investigate the world of clinical psychology. There are many populations who use the services of a clinical psychologist. Perhaps Ana would be more suited to working with a different group of people with other issues. While her vision of clinical psychology doesn't exist in the real world, she might be able to conjure another, truer vision. She may also need to look at entirely different career venues to discover her calling. Achieving these insights and discoveries will all take some time—time beyond graduation.

Common Threads

So what do we see when we look at these stories? Each person goes through a seismic shift in the way he/she sees and makes sense of the world. The shift affects how they think, feel, act, and relate to others. Each must cope with his/her ambivalence about leaving the safe and the known. Each must learn to live with the ambiguity that's left when one gives up the notion that "the answer" exists. Each must suffer. Each must learn to trust the journey.

SHARON DALOZ PARKS
ON YOUNG ADULTHOOD

Sharon Daloz Parks (2000) has focused her research on the search for faith and meaning in the world. She is a strong advocate of redefining developmental stages to include "young adult." She casts this developmental period as a time when twenty-somethings are tentatively but tenaciously recognizing and learning to value their own voices and their own inner authority. Young adults make meaning by "becoming critically aware of one's own composing reality, self-consciously participating in an ongoing dialogue toward truth, and cultivating a capacity to respond—to act—in ways that are satisfying and just" (p. 6). In short, young adults are called upon to actively and consciously create the life they want to live. They are challenged to take ownership of their lives by discovering their own answers to life's big questions. Ultimately they must make life choices that are congruent with the meaning they have created for themselves. Changing their beliefs about what is true and real in the world is no small task. Parks suggests that young adults may have contradictory feelings about the experience. On one hand, they may feel redeemed, relieved, or even thrilled by their brave new world. They may also feel vulnerable and uncertain, however, as they reconfigure their relationships and deal with the discrepancies between the claims of the world and the claims of the self. Parks states that, ". . . along the way there is also some measure of challenge, threat, bewilderment, frustration, anxiety, loss, emptiness, or other suffering. In other words, there may be some element of shipwreck . . ." (p. 71).

Shipwreck, Gladness, and Amazement

"Shipwreck" is Parks' term for a developmental crisis. A shipwreck changes everything. The world as it was no longer exists. Initially there is nothing to replace what has been lost and no obvious means of survival. This powerful word seems a precise characterization of the experiences of young adulthood. Parks explains,

> Metaphorical shipwreck may occur with the loss of relationship, violence to one's property, collapse of a career venture, physical illness or injury, defeat of a cause, a fateful choice that irrevocably reorders one's life, betrayal by a community or government, or the discovery that an intellectual construct is inadequate. Sometimes we simply encounter someone, or some new experience or idea, that calls into question things as we have perceived them, or as they were taught to us, or as we had read, heard, or assumed. This kind of experience can suddenly rip into the fabric of life, or it may slowly yet just as surely unravel the meanings that have served as the home of the soul (p. 28).

We can look at the stories of Karen, Jim, and Ana and find the place of shipwreck. For Karen, the point at which medical school became a reality instead of a distant goal caused her shipwreck. For Ana it was the experience of her internship. Jim experienced shipwreck more than once. Finding a job after graduation was his first experience with shipwreck; leaving the community he had established in AmeriCorps was his second.

Karen and Jim were not only able to survive their difficult experiences, but were able to thrive. Karen found a career that incorporated her math and her artistic abilities. Jim's AmeriCorps experience taught him that he had many options rather than one, right choice. He learned to test out new opportunities—sticking with things he found satisfying and letting go of things that didn't hold his interest or enthusiasm. Parks refers to this ability to appreciate a new and improved world as "gladness."

> It is gladness that pervades one's whole being; there is a new sense of vitality, be it quiet or exuberant. Usually, however, there is more than relief in this gladness. There is transformation. We discover a new reality beyond the loss. Rarely, are we able to replace, to completely recompose, what was before. The loss of earlier meaning is irretrievable and must be grieved and mourned. But gladness arises from the discovery that life continues to

unfold with meaning, with connections of significance and delight . . . (it) is experienced, in part, as a new knowing. Though this knowing sometimes comes at the price of real tragedy (which even the new knowing does not justify), we typically would not wish to return to the ignorance that preceded coming to the new shore. We do not want to live in a less-adequate truth, a less viable sense of reality, an insufficient wisdom (p. 29).

Ana has not had the experience of gladness yet. Her shipwreck is fresh, and she is still stinging with the loss of her career dream. She has not yet acquired enough new knowledge or experience to value the difficulty she now faces. But she will.

According to Parks, gladness and amazement go hand-in-hand. "The power of the experience of shipwreck is located precisely in one's inability to immediately sense the promise of anything beyond the breakup of what has been secure and trustworthy . . . Then, when we are met by the surprise of new meaning, we are amazed" (p. 31). Most people have had the experience of looking back over a difficult period in their lives and being "amazed" that they got through it. They are also "amazed" to discover that those particularly difficult periods spawned tremendous change and growth.

Howdy, Pilgrim!—Tools to Make the Journey

"A good life and the cultivation of wisdom require a balance of home and pilgrimage" (p. 51). Parks defines "home" as a genuinely safe place of belonging. Every young adult must have a "home"—a comforting, welcoming, supportive place to rest and recharge. "Pilgrimage" may be a literal or symbolic journey, a leave-taking that is necessary for any young adult who seeks to stake a claim on his or her own identity. While everyone's journey is unique, there are also common elements that can assist the young adult traveler.

Heed the Signs The world sends you information all the time. Observe. Listen. Look for patterns. Gregg Levoy (1997) suggests: "Make a tally of the signals you've been receiving around any given issue—through dreams, fantasies, cravings and ambitions, persistent symptoms, the fears and resistances that have been preoccupying you lately, any opportunity whose sudden appearance in your life borders on synchronicity . . ." (p. 37). For example, how would you interpret the fact that a person has rejected the idea of an artistic career, but keeps running into people who are making a living using their art? If you allow it into your awareness, you will discover that the world often shoves you, sometimes relentlessly, in the direction of your true self. All you have to do is be open to the messages that are being sent your way.

Participate in Community Find and become a part of a community—people who share examined perspectives. Community can be found in the obvious (church group, volunteer organization, alumni association) or not-so-obvious (book club, sailing lessons, yoga class) places. Belong to a culture of care, both for the individual and the group. A community can reduce the vulnerability you feel and support you as you discern what is true and just.

Challenge Yourself Interact with and appreciate people who are not like you. Explore "otherness" by learning to live across boundaries of geography, culture, race, age, etc. Study or work abroad. Volunteer for a ministry immersion trip to another part of the country. Take a cooking class that focuses on food from a culture other than your own. Experience one new thing every day and consider that a thing worth doing is worth doing badly!

Form a Dream Examine the your own calling (see chapter 8). Believe in something larger than yourself. Develop a personal mission statement and then work toward making it real. Walk the talk.

GRADUATION AS COMMENCEMENT

Most college students go through the developmental period of young adulthood exactly as they are meant to—with anxiety, trepidation, confusion about the ambiguity of life, and ambivalence about whom they are and what they should be doing. College graduation is much more about beginning than ending. We attend a "commencement ceremony" to celebrate what is about to start as well as what has been accomplished.

In the first few pages of this chapter, we spoke about Matthew and Andrew. Matthew's college graduation produced a very real shipwreck. It took him the better part of 18 months to begin to make some meaning of his life. His first step was to find a job. He didn't like the work much, but he was well regarded, developed some colleagues, and started to pay some bills. He also began to take better care of his physical self. Fourteen months after that, he looked better, felt better, and was great company once again. He decided to find a new job that was more in line with his interests and abilities and applied for a highly competitive position. He began that job about a year ago and started graduate school in the fall. He says it is just recently that he feels as though he has come out on the other side. He is indeed amazed that he survived and grateful to be where he is right now. He also recognizes that he could not have gotten to this place without having gone through the shipwreck. While he didn't enjoy what happened, he does understand and appreciate it.

As for Andrew, he is on his way to graduate school now, having been through a shipwreck of his own. While the word "adult" probably doesn't come to mind every time he looks in the mirror, it is not as foreign a concept as it once was. It seems important to share the end of the conversation Andrew and his mother had while driving back to school.

Understanding his anxiety about growing up, she replied, "No one becomes an adult all at once. There is no particular moment of passage when adulthood descends upon you. Growing up is a process. Perfection is not required; as a matter of fact, mistakes are expected. Make them, learn from them, and move on. You are not required to do everything; you just have to be willing to do the next thing."

And while you're at it, try to enjoy the journey!

JOURNAL STARTERS

1. Use Marcia's work to name and describe your identity status when you first entered college. How has it fluctuated over time? What is your current identity status?

2. If you weren't worried about the consequences, what change would you introduce into your life right now to help you evolve?

3. How have you been shipwrecked? How has the experience changed your reality?

4. What are your thoughts on, "A thing worth doing is worth doing badly."?

FYI

- *http://evoke.luc.edu/index.html,* EVOKE, a Loyola University Chicago project focused on calling

- *www.inventuregroup.com,* Richard Leider, principal, consulting group that helps people put purpose to work in their personal and professional lives

- *www.marybold.com/CogFunc.htm,* identifies the researchers and key terms linked to cognitive functioning in early adulthood

- *www.soulfulliving.com,* guide for personal and spiritual growth that focuses on a new topic each month

REFERENCES

Chickering, A. W. (1969). *Education and identity.* San Francisco: Jossey-Bass.

Chickering, A. W. and Reisser, L. (1993). *Education and identity.* (2nd ed.). San Francisco: Jossey-Bass.

Cramer, C., Flynn, B. and LaFave, A. (1997). *Erik Erikson's 8 stages of psychosocial development. www.facultyweb.cortland.edu/~ANDERSMD/ERIK/welcome.HTML*

Evans, N. J., Forney, D. S. and Guido-DiBrito, F. (1998). *Student development in college: Theory, research, and practice.* San Francisco: Jossey-Bass.

Levoy, G. (1997). *Callings: Finding and following an authentic life.* New York: Three Rivers Press.

McAdams, D. P. (2001). *The person: An integrated approach to personality psychology.* Orlando, FL: Harcourt, Inc.

Mountain Dreamer, O. (1999). *The invitation.* San Francisco: HarperCollins. 1999.

Parks, S. D. (2000). *Big questions, worthy dreams.* San Francisco: Jossey-Bass.

Parks, S. D. (2002). "Big-Enough Questions." Speech presented at Loyola University Chicago, Chicago, IL.

4

≋

Cognitive Development During and After College

What You Should Know About Knowing

Education is the process of moving from cocksure ignorance to thoughtful uncertainty.

SOURCE UNKNOWN

It's the first class in an interdisciplinary course about issues relating to the 9/11 attacks. Because the department chair wants this course to be accessible to all levels of students, the instructor consents to admitting freshmen through seniors. While she explains the syllabus, a few students ask questions about the term paper assignment, including the following. "I'm a science major. Is it okay if I emphasize technological perspectives in my paper?" Another student inquires, "To what extent can we analyze and evaluate the readings rather than simply summarize them?" A third student asks, "How many pages long is it supposed to be; how many references do you want; and what topic will you assign us to write about?" When the instructor mentions that 30 percent of the final grade is based on student participation and small group discussion, one student remarks to his classmate, "Why is so much of the grade based on student input? I'm paying tuition to hear experts lecture, not to hear students talk." But another student replies, "Thirty percent for participation? I think it's cool that the teacher believes we can learn from each other."

Some student remarks reflect a more sophisticated *level of knowing* and understanding the syllabus than others. The person who complained about the 30 percent participation component *assumes* that the knowledge to be gained from the course resides in the expertise and authority of the instructor, whereas the student who replied *assumes* that peers can contribute to learning. The student who asked about page length, number of references, and topic assignment *assumes* they are the critical parts of the paper. The science major and the student who inquired about analysis and evaluation *assume* that connecting the material to particular contexts are key factors. Can you explain which remarks may have been expressed by a typical freshman and which by a senior?

Most students are neither aware of the assumptions they hold about the process of knowing, nor that these assumptions change throughout early adulthood, shaping what and how they learn, inside and outside the classroom. Many students do not realize *the patterns of knowing they develop in college often collide with the reality of knowing and learning in the workplace.* This chapter describes the levels of cognitive development that emerge during college, the drastic changes in knowing that occur in the workplace, and steps you can take to monitor and advance your assumptions about knowing. A caveat is in order. You will be introduced to several new concepts in order to understand the fascinating but subtle ways your intellect interacts with your world. Be patient and persistent, and you will acquire extremely valuable suggestions for your post-college years that you can implement well before graduation.

BAXTER MAGOLDA'S FOUR
STAGES OF KNOWING

In 1986 Marcia Baxter Magolda began a unique, highly acclaimed, longitudinal study of 101 college freshmen (51 women and 50 men). From the interviews and questionnaire data she collected, Baxter Magolda uncovered four discernible levels of knowing: (1) absolute, (2) transitional, (3) independent, and (4) contextual (Baxter Magolda 1992). Knowing about knowing enables you to understand how you and others approach situations that require a particular level of thinking and problem solving. Advancement through each level is characterized by changes in students' progressively more complex beliefs regarding the certainty of knowledge and the roles of authority, self, and peers in the process of knowing.

Absolute Knowing

In the first stage, *absolute knowing,* students believe that knowledge is certain and that absolute answers exist in all areas. Ideas are right or wrong, good or bad; there is nothing in between. Students expect the all-knowing professor to serve as an intellectual banker who transfers truths from her "knowledge account" to theirs. The absolute knower approaches a course by assuming that the teacher and the textbook—*the* authorities, *the* experts—have *the* answers to the issues being studied. Absolute knowers believe that their job is to attend class, take notes, memorize, and reproduce (regurgitate?) the knowledge in the next exam or paper. They are often passive learners who expect the teacher to provide the structure and make all the decisions including (recalling the previous example), the term paper topic and the number of pages and references. Unfortunately many teachers reinforce absolute knowing by over-structuring their courses and their answers to such questions. In non-academic situations, the absolute knower might assume that there are certain, ready-made solutions for common problems, whether it is the peer who plays music too loudly, the club meeting that seems poorly conducted, or the job supervisor who fails to provide clear and immediate answers to each question.

Transitional Knowing

Transitional knowing serves as a transition between the perceived certainty of absolute knowing and the high level of uncertainty characteristic of independent knowing. As a transitional knower, you begin to question the certainty of knowledge and the authorities that convey it because you are discovering that some truths are not as certain as they appear. Not everything can be easily categorized as right or wrong, good or evil; there are gray areas. You recognize the existence of multiple perspectives, even contradictions. Theorists disagree; knowledge is complex. If knowledge seems uncertain in this stage, it is because authorities have not yet found a certain answer—but they will. You believe the instructor's role is to help you understand information so you do not have to rely on rote memory to acquire knowledge. For example, the transitional knower enrolled in Microeconomics may doubt the experts when theories fail to account for current market conditions and then ask the teacher for an explanation. The student whose best friend claims unfair treatment by a residence hall judicial board's complaints of loud music could question the board's objectivity, the friend's honesty, or the policy. For the transitional knower, peers still are not sources of knowledge, but they can help by participating in class discussions and exchanging views.

Independent Knowing

In the third stage, *independent knowing*, knowledge is viewed as mostly uncertain. As an independent knower you discover there are fewer absolute truths and more ambiguities than you previously believed. Your worldviews are changing. Because knowledge is uncertain, you believe multiple perspectives exist on an issue. Truth appears to be relative, i.e., "It depends." Teachers and textbooks are no longer *the* authorities. You may be quick to question or criticize experts and assert that, since there are no correct answers, your opinions are as valid as theirs. The problem with this stance is that you might not seek evidence to support your views, a failure that often collides with the expectations of authorities (teachers, administrators, employers, loved ones) that demand evidence. Although as an independent knower you are beginning to think for yourself and *construct* knowledge from your experiences, you may also want your peers to share opinions and serve as a source of knowledge. Thus the role of peers in the knowing process becomes more important with each stage.

Contextual Knowing

In *contextual knowing,* you become aware that knowledge is mostly uncertain, but you realize that some claims to knowledge are better than others *if* evidence exists to support them *relative* to a particular situation. Contextual knowers enjoy thinking through issues, comparing differing perspectives critically, integrating new with existing knowledge, and applying it to new contexts (Baxter Magolda 1992). As a contextual knower you must deal with complex issues that require that you critically examine different perspectives and make decisions based on evidence. Such issues are wide-ranging and might include: remaining in an unhealthy relationship, choosing a major you enjoy vs. one that leads to a good job, having friends whose lifestyles contradict your value system, remaining on a team where the coach is strongly biased, deciding if the death penalty is always wrong, or deciding if a war is justified.

Recall the scenario that opened this chapter. The science major in the 9/11 class who wants to emphasize technology and the student who inquired about analyzing and evaluating the material are thinking contextually. The first student seeks to integrate new information with existing knowledge and apply it. The second student wants to think through the issues and compare ideas according to evaluative criteria. Similarly, loud music may be more tolerable on a spring break in a relatively empty residence hall than in the middle of the night during final exam week.

THE COURSE OF COGNITIVE GROWTH
FROM COLLEGE TO CAREER

At this point you may think that Baxter Magolda's model is an interesting intellectual exercise, but don't her four stages really reflect the differences between freshman, sophomore, junior, and senior years? NO! It's not that simple.

First, you learned in your social science courses that research studies are conducted within a particular context of procedures and sampling domains and may not be generalized to everyone. Such caveats apply here, and we will return to these issues later. In addition the four levels of cognitive development do not correspond to the four milestones in college. Figure 4.1 shows that absolute knowing dominates the first year and that transitional knowing characterizes the second, third, and fourth years. Independent knowing was the predominant mode for only 1% of the sophomores, 5% of the juniors, and 16% of seniors. Contextual knowing was observed in only 1% and 2% of the juniors and seniors, respectively. Are these statistics good or bad news? Perhaps both. Notice that absolute knowing declines markedly each year to where it

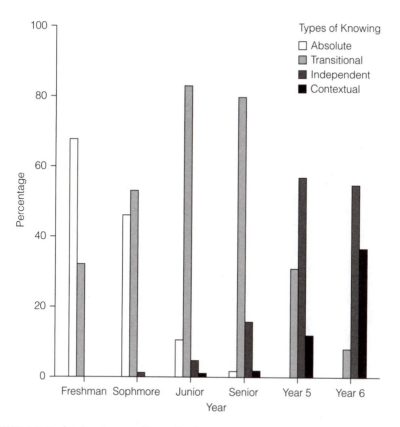

FIGURE 4.1 Predominant ways of knowing by year

SOURCES: From Baxter Magolda, M. B. (1992). *Knowing and reasoning in students: Gender-related patterns in students' intellectual development.* Copyright © 1992 Jossey-Bass. Material is used with permission from John Wiley and Sons, Inc.
Baxter Magolda, M. B. (1994). Post-college experiences and epistemology. *The Review of Higher Education,* 18(1): 25–44. Copyright The Association for the Study of Higher Education. Reprinted with permission of the John Hopkins University Press.

characterizes only 2% of the seniors. Thus after four years of college, students in this sample learned that authorities do not have *the* answers because there are usually multiple perspectives amid so many uncertainties and different situations. For example, you may realize that that art, business, nursing, science, sociology, and other academic majors are highly developed, complex fields each with contrasting perspectives and applications. Similarly you may have learned that living with a roommate, holding a job, constructing your identity, maintaining healthy relationships, succeeding in a career, managing a family, and other dimensions of everyday living are complex, uncertain endeavors with few, if any, easy answers. If you have learned during college to shift your dependence from authorities to yourself and simultaneously recognize that life has more uncertainties than you earlier thought, that is good news!

Review Figure 4.1 again and notice that transitional knowing rapidly replaces absolute knowing as the dominant mode of learning, especially during the junior and senior years. In fact many students are stuck in transitional knowing when they graduate. For example, as a transitional knower you may question authorities and acknowledge uncertainties, but you may not be thinking independently, not using others as resources, not comparing multiple perspectives, not seeking evidence to support your claims, and not developing your own voice. You may be acquiring *information* from coursework, but your *assumptions* about knowing are not growing more complex. Some people would argue that being stuck in transitional knowing at graduation is bad news, especially if you assume that your intellectual growth peaks as you complete college. Baxter Magolda's findings imply that most students will have achieved only the first two levels of knowing when they receive their diploma. The level achieved is not necessarily due to individual limitations because, however, it may be that the students were not sufficiently challenged by their educational experiences.

Several factors may contribute to most students' tendency to remain in transitional knowing, including the failure in some educational environments to promote independent and contextual knowing, the unwillingness of many students to accept academic and personal growth challenges, and the entry into that new and vast body of knowledge that comprises the academic major (more expectations of certainty?). Instead of speculating why most students do not graduate as independent or contextual knowers, it is more productive if we ask why these two levels increase drastically after college (see Figure 4.1) and why transitional knowing drops out. Subsequently we will identify specific steps you can take that may accelerate (but we aren't certain!) your cognitive growth *and prepare you for post-college settings where facility with higher levels of knowing is expected.*

After the students in Baxter Magolda's study entered the work force or graduate school, independent knowing rapidly increased to 57 percent and 55 percent during the fifth and sixth years, respectively, while contextual knowing improved from 12 percent to 37 percent, respectively, during this time. That's great progress! What happened after graduation to account for the rapid growth? Baxter Magolda conducted post-college interviews with 70 of her original 101 participants during the fifth year of the study and with 51 participants during the sixth year (Baxter Magolda 1994). Most graduates had accepted jobs in such areas as insurance, sales, accounting, teaching, mental health, airlines, and government; others had entered graduate or professional school.

Themes of Independent Knowers

Three themes emerged from her interviews with independent knowers that appear to account for their growth. First, as employees they were expected to *function independently.* For instance, an individual in the insurance field identified her employer's expectations of independent functioning this way,

"They say, Here's your desk; . . . here's your phone; here's the mailbox. Here's a little bit of clientele to get started. Start your own business. Here's some suggested ways to do it. Here's the people who have done it and been successful. But this isn't necessarily the way you have to do it. See if you can build yourself a business" (Baxter Magolda 1994, p. 32). To develop independence, it is important to have room to think, evaluate, make decisions, and act on feedback from your work. The quotation above exemplifies the room some employees are given. Many aspects of the college environment promote independence, and most teachers design instruction to foster independence in various ways. Often such activities and attitudes are neither articulated clearly by educators (e.g., "This course . . . teaches you to think and act independently in these ways. . . .") nor heard by students. *Remember, there are no syllabi in the workplace that list weekly assignments, due dates, and office hours.*

The second characteristic of the independent knowers was the requirement to learn their job by learning from others, to *use peers as sources of information and models.* A recreational therapist acknowledged that theme this way, "I open myself up to other people to learn from them. They are my second greatest asset. I look at things they do, evaluate that in my mind, and make a decision about what I can take from it. I learn from our fine arts director, people outside the recreational program, people on the residential unit." (Baxter Magolda 1994, p. 32). The transitional knowing assumption that peers are unimportant in the learning process is no longer valid in the workplace. From their peers and superiors, new employees learn an array of phenomena including specific task-related skills as well as norms and policies of the organizations' culture. Recall Holton's taxonomy of new employee learning tasks presented in chapter 2.

The third theme was the role of *direct experience.* One participant commented about the work reviewed in her performance evaluation, "I learned how to become very clear and concise . . . I learned to be prepared. I learned that you don't call someone when you don't know what you're talking about. You learn those things in school, but you don't really experience them. *You don't experience the consequences or you don't experience the reality.*" (emphasis added) (Baxter Magolda 1994, p. 33). The graduates maintained that direct, hands-on experience with a particular situation enabled them to make decisions about how to function. Typically students learn *vicariously* through teachers and textbooks, but a true understanding of the task is constructed in a particular context or situation. For example, an accounting student may receive an "A" for learning procedures taught in class, but that person will master accounting procedures better in a job. The diagnostic categories of dysfunctional child behavior are studied in a child behavior disorders course, but comprehensive knowledge is constructed from years of experiences as a special education teacher. The geography major better understands rapid over-development of rural areas adjacent to large cities through field visits, even if prior classroom instruction was superior.

Themes of Contextual Knowers

Three major themes emerged from interviews with contextual knowers that could explain the important increases from 1 percent and 2 percent during the junior and senior years, respectively, to 12 percent and 37 percent during the first two years after college. First, contextual knowers were frequently required to *make subjective decisions* involving uncertainties. Consider the ambiguities faced by the real estate leaser (and recent college graduate). "The way I go into it now is I just use what I know and then I get a feel for the situation and then I pretty much know what I have to ask or find out." (Baxter Magolda 1994, p. 36). Gone is the absolute knowing assumption that certain answers exist and the authorities have them. Gone is the transitional knowing assumption that some uncertainties exist and it is just a matter of time before *the* answers are found. This individual (and most new college graduates) works in a position where uncertainty in decision-making is the rule, not the exception.

Contextual knowers were also in positions that offered them *independence and authority,* primarily authority over their own schedule. As one participant attested, "I'm in the office one day a week and the rest of the time I'm on my own. I have a company car, car phone, laptop computer. I pretty much work out of my house the rest of the days . . . I'm more independent. I have full authority for everything I do." (Baxter Magolda 1994, p. 36). Having authority over others is another common experience for recent graduates who serve in manager or assistant manager positions in retail stores or various office environments. Although organizational structures and reporting hierarchies are usually defined, most positions include uncertain and unpredictable situations in the day-to-day decision making, prioritizing of work, and interaction with co-workers and customers.

The third theme revealed by contextual knowers is *collaboration* with co-workers, especially in the exchange of ideas. One law student remarked, "Hopefully you're going to have people of different opinions so that you can have a sounding board and they can question you and you can question them and so on. I think [that] through this I will be able to come up with some better understanding of the topic. I might change my views, might keep them the same, might make them stronger. Those types of things encourage forming a more cohesive, better informed view." (Baxter Magolda 1994, p. 38). Such comments indicate that collaboration is performed not simply to gather information, but to exchange ideas and work effectively. The interviews revealed additional themes: self-confidence with a "can do" attitude that stretches one's limits; the conviction that individuals were contributing to the organization, not just collecting a paycheck; and the insight that constructing personal meaning from work is an important dimension in life.

What about Graduate School?

Baxter Magolda was interested in the experiences of 12 women and 13 men who continued their education in graduate or professional programs in psychology, economics, education, business administration, international relations, law, pre-medicine, seminary, or art history, or who enrolled in courses preparatory to graduate school, banking, or real estate.

Several major interrelated themes or values emerged from the interviews. First, many professors encouraged students to explore and struggle with ideas as a means of establishing their own positions, thinking for themselves, and constructing knowledge. Second, students benefited from forming connections among life experiences, knowledge, and their sense of identity, provided that the academic environments were designed to make these dimensions central to learning. Students who enrolled in graduate programs directly connected to their jobs, such as business, social work, computer science, and education, to name a few, often experienced these satisfying inter-connections when instructors skillfully incorporated their knowledge and experiences into papers, projects, exams, journals, and other assignments. Third, learning environments in which there was mutual respect and equality in student-instructor relationships were highly valued (Baxter Magolda 1996).

WHAT YOU CAN DO *NOW*

How can you apply this information between now and the time you graduate? There are no magic solutions that guarantee a quick trip to contextual knowing (It's absolute knowing to expect any!), but there are steps that you can take in the academic and co-curricular aspects of your college experience as well as in your "other life" that help prepare you for "the real world."

Your Academic Environment

In the Classroom Most courses you take fulfill either core/distribution or major requirements; your electives offer you greater freedom to choose. Whether your coursework and instructors have been chosen for you or by you, pay close attention to the assignments and methods of instruction. Recognize that the nature of some course material, class size, and teaching style may require a predominantly *teacher-centered* course—one where communication is mostly top-down and few opportunities exist to interact with the instructor, other students, or the material. Some courses are lecture-oriented so that students master essential technical information, but there should still be opportunities for active involvement with the material, including student input. In contrast, certain courses are predominantly *student-centered*. Communication is generally interactive among students and instructor, and assignments often draw upon student interests and experiences. In some seminar courses the topic may serve mainly as a catalyst for student involvement, the teacher's primary agenda. In general, student-centered courses provide good opportunities for cognitive growth. How does this occur? Recall the themes attributed to the independent and contextual knower in Baxter Magolda's post-college study as you examine the following suggestions.

1. Participate Teachers who expect participation in class discussion or small groups are not simply policing your class preparation habits. They are creating opportunities for you to understand the material (beyond exams and papers), think independently, connect ideas to your knowledge and experiences (contexts), and create public identity with the issues (you publicly defend your beliefs). Small group discussions that focus on case studies, problem solving, and thought-provoking questions enable you to communicate your ideas and learn from your peers. Formal or informal individual or team debates are an excellent venue in which to gather and present evidence, defend a particular position, and rebut opponents.

The risks in thoughtful participation are many: expressing ideas that are strange to some peers, defending your beliefs, opening yourself to criticism, and responding to the uncertainty of the situation. Ultimately, *you must decide* if it is better to take such risks in the relatively supportive environment of a college classroom and subsequently learn from your experience or delay such learning until later in the work place when a performance evaluation or a job may hinge on your ability to communicate and defend your ideas. In intelligent participation (Not all participation is intelligent!), everybody benefits. Shyness, lack of preparation, or apathy (the most common reasons for remaining silent) are not marketable skills. After all, when was the last time you saw a job opening for someone highly experienced in passivity and silence?

2. Analyze your written assignments Professors are neither sadists nor masochists. The next time you get grumpy about a paper the instructor assigned, just remember that, although you have to write it, the teacher reads and grades it—and those of everyone else in class. Consequently, there must be a reason for the teacher's "cruelty." Major papers typically require that you summarize, analyze, and compare different perspectives. End-of-class or short essay papers assume many forms, but often they seek your reactions, understanding, or evaluation of ideas or issues. Journals and logs assess your ability to express ideas and connect them to course concepts or specific experiences (contexts). As a positive challenge, welcome assignments that call upon your experiences (whatever they may be), challenge your beliefs, require evidence to support convictions, and promote connections to other aspects of your life. Such assignments may be difficult, but they empower you to go beyond the absolute and transitional forms of knowing (dependence on authorities, expectations of certain answers) and think independently in particular contexts using evidence to support your views.

3. Don't regard a test simply as a test Your professors employ several strategies to assess learning, but the most familiar and feared method is the test. Carefully constructed exams (including multiple choice) challenge students to think at advanced levels of knowing. One way to determine if an exam measures knowing at higher or lower levels is to focus on verbs contained in the questions or item stems. Take a few minutes with your dictionary (Don't wing it!) and briefly define each of the familiar terms contained in the list below. Enter key words of the definition and then indicate if the verb reflects assumptions about knowing primarily at the lower (absolute, transitional) or higher (independent, contextual) levels. Briefly justify your choices.

Verb	Key Words of Definition	Level of Knowing
Define		
Compare		
Evaluate		
Describe		
Apply		
Design		
Name		
Explain		
Contrast		
Create		
List		
Illustrate		
Synthesize		

Some of the verbs above do not clearly fit into one or the other levels of knowing (Does that uncertainty bother you?), depending upon the contexts in which they are used. Most (more uncertainty!) teachers would agree that "define," "describe," "name," and "list" instruct the student to repeat information or demonstrate understanding, however, verbs such as "explain," "compare," "evaluate," "design," "contrast," "synthesize," and "create" instruct students to think beyond the recitation and comprehension of material. What about verbs such as "apply" and "illustrate"? It depends on whether the instructor wants textbook and lecture examples (which require repetition or comprehension) or original examples (which require connections to ideas and reflect higher level knowing). It depends!

Off-Campus Study Programs One of the most productive growth opportunities is an off-campus study program. Typically students spend a term or school year abroad in a foreign country. However, some colleges in rural areas operate off-campus programs in a metropolitan area; others afford students the chance to work or study in rural America. Regardless of the setting, off-campus study programs are great opportunities for intellectual and personal growth. Recall the themes that characterize the post-college independent and contextual knower, and consider how they may apply to a person (to yourself!) who elects an academic term or year in Africa, Asia, Australia, Europe, or South America. Until you become familiar with the setting and the culture, you are faced with numerous *uncertainties* on a daily basis. In the absence of familiar *authorities,* you will depend on your own judgment, often in *ambiguous* situations.

You will likely seek opinions of *peers* and other strangers as you daily navigate (*direct experience*) the language, culture, customs, educational institution, religion, and politics of the host country. You function relatively *independently,* serve as *the authority* over your actions, and make many *subjective decisions* in unfamiliar *contexts.* Sometimes you take risks, make mistakes, offend others, and make bad decisions. Other times you are ecstatic about your adventure, pleased with your wise decisions, meet fascinating people, open your mind to *other perspectives,* and reflect on the many positive aspects of this experience. Many students regard study abroad as financially prohibitive. Before you draw this conclusion, however, be sure to investigate the programs available and compare the costs of living on campus with those that you would incur studying abroad. The difference may not be as great as you think. Most students return from a term abroad with vastly improved maturity, self-confidence, and openness to experience. For some, it is the highlight of their college education.

Service Learning, Internships, and Other Experiential Learning Opportunities Many employers value significant experiential activities because learning in the workplace occurs more by performance than through study. Furthermore, it is not uncommon for students who have performed exceptionally to receive a job offer as the internship ends. Many graduate schools use service learning, internships, or extra-course research experiences as a litmus test of an applicant's readiness. Nearly all colleges and universities offer some form of experiential learning, required or optional, credit-based or voluntary. Check with your academic department, student activities, career planning, or similar offices. There are usually several opportunities available to become involved—not just once but as often as your schedule permits. Just as study abroad can stimulate higher levels of knowing, so too can certain experiential learning activities, as Case in Point 4.1 indicates.

Not every internship or service learning experience presents the challenges Alexis faced. Sometimes students spend too much time performing menial or routine work. Routine is part of most jobs, and it is important to recognize and experience its reality. When interviewing for credit-based internships or service learning projects, however, students should inquire about the variety and level of tasks to be performed, supervision and feedback, and the learning outcomes they are likely to experience.

This chapter focuses on the role of experiential learning in cognitive development, however, do not overlook the immense benefits of service learning, internships, and volunteer work for stimulating personal growth, altruism, value clarification, community involvement, and cultural awareness. Finally, many employers and graduate or professional schools will expect to see experiential learning activities reflected on your resume.

Get Involved Your instructors are not simply subject matter specialists whose lives are confined to their classrooms, labs, or offices. Most are approachable, even when they are busy; many *enjoy* spending time with students. If you have questions about a course, the discipline, or careers, sign up for an appointment. If they do not have the time or interest in you, they will

CASE IN POINT 4.1   Contextual Knowing in a Social Service Agency

Alexis was a college senior in her mid-twenties who wanted a credit-based internship in a social services agency to test her interest in a counseling or social work field. After researching several agencies, she chose to interview at a shelter for abused women that operated in a suburb of a major city. Alexis prepared well for the interview, and her application was accepted. She arranged with her supervisor to work at the agency approximately three hours a day for three days a week during the 14-week semester. Alexis received several hours of training that included listening and communication skills, information about domestic violence, familiarization with agency policies and state laws, and the types and locations of various resources available to the callers (her clients). Her main responsibility was to respond to phone calls and consult the center's staff with questions she could not answer. As some calls were from women seeking shelter, Alexis was responsible for screening the call, recommending if the woman seeking help should be admitted to the center, and identifying the resources (e.g., medical, police, pastoral) to be contacted.

The internship provided Alexis with considerable knowledge and insights about abused women and the circumstances that brought them in contact with the center. She benefited from the mentoring of a dedicated staff that included a social worker, legal specialist, and administrator. She learned to handle significant responsibilities in stressful situations. The internship was a significant growth experience for her. The supervisor and staff were highly pleased with her work and would have offered her a position had funds been available.

To what extent did her experience parallel those of Baxter Magolda's post-college participants?

Direct experience in a particular context: Alexis' training, responsibilities, and interaction with clients and staff generated a solid understanding of a serious social problem in this particular setting that could not have been matched by the vicarious learning achieved in a classroom. Still her prior coursework was a necessary academic preparation for the internship.

Learning from others and collaboration: Alexis learned about her work from diverse professional staff during the initial training and often depended on them and other resources in order to assist her clients/callers. From her clients she learned first hand about many aspects of domestic violence.

Functioning independently, acting as an authority, and making subjective decisions in ambiguous situations: Following her training, Alexis was expected to function independently and act as an authority, yet she was encouraged to consult the staff when it was necessary. Due to the different situations and needs of her clients, the stress and pain they were experiencing, and the uncertainties surrounding their situation, she often made decisions that were partially or highly subjective, even though she operated from the guidelines provided during her training sessions.

In short, Alexis' internship was an intense exposure (for nine hours each week) to a serious social problem; her responsibilities and experiences stretched her assumptions about knowing. Were she a business intern

(Continued)

CASE IN POINT 4.1   Continued

working for an investment firm, a nursing student in an oncology unit, a special education student teacher, an engineering intern in a computer company, or in many other settings, she could have faced analogous challenges. Did Alexis' experiences cause her to become a contextual knower? Not likely, but it helped.

Had she stayed full-time and faced similar or more complex challenges over a period of one or two years, her characteristic mode of knowing could have reached the contextual level. (There are too many unknowns and uncertainties to provide you with a certain answer to this question).

let you know, but don't take a rejection personally. Ask about research projects or activities in which they are engaged. Most teachers enjoy discussing their professional interests. According to Alexander Astin (1999), involvement (with courses, teachers, and peers) has a powerful influence on promoting a student's cognitive and emotional development. It is not unusual for a student to enjoy a particular instructor immensely, subsequently enroll in other classes she or he teaches, complete an independent study or internship with the teacher, and subsequently pursue graduate school or a career in the area of the instructor's expertise. In short, some teachers act as mentors and have a powerful influence on your life. It takes the right chemistry for both parties; but if the chemistry is right, the life of the student and the instructor can be greatly affected. One of the best forms of involvement is with staff, peers, and faculty through your college's co-curriculum.

Cognitive Development and the Co-Curriculum

Years of schooling have conditioned us to think that the most important learning experiences occur in the classroom. Often they do, however, college consists of two curriculums. The *overt* curriculum is contained in the catalog of courses, reflected in the knowledge you acquire, and recorded on your transcripts. College also includes a *covert* curriculum, "those numerous, routine skill-related activities, behaviors, and attitudes that are transacted inside and outside of classrooms" (Hettich 1998). The covert curriculum consists of such life/learning strategies as interpersonal communications, time and stress management, habits of responsibility, self-discipline, and study skills, to name a few. For example, your communication, especially with individuals who are different from you, leads to exchanging information, opinions, and beliefs at progressively deeper levels of disclosure. It affords continuing opportunities to compare and contrast ideas, become open to multiple perspectives, clarify values, and understand the special contexts in which other people live. Similarly, when you act responsibly in your relationships with peers, supervisors, teachers, employers, and family members, you build strong collaborative networks. When you participate in your institution's co-curriculum you cultivate habits of higher level knowing. (Baxter Magolda 1992).

Most colleges and universities display enough diversity in their co-curricular offerings to attract even the most discriminating students. Students join co-curricular activities to enjoy a break from coursework, have fun, gain knowledge and skills, and develop new relationships. After you feel comfortable in a particular club, team, or other group, consider seeking a leadership position that suits your skills and interests. Skilled student leaders operate as managers, given the diverse responsibilities, tasks, and human interaction involved. For example, think of a group or activity that you are familiar with and use the checklist below to ascertain the tasks the leaders perform or should perform.

Leaders:

_____ plan and conduct meetings

_____ are responsible for particular tasks, e.g., producing a newspaper, planning, and conducting events

_____ work with other members to satisfy the needs of the group

_____ are responsible for operating under budget constraints

_____ periodically meet with a group sponsor or staff member

_____ interact with individuals who are different from them

_____ perform public relations, promote events

_____ work with vendors or other services

_____ manage the activities of other students, directly or indirectly

_____ operate under pressure while carrying a full academic load, a job, or other significant responsibilities

Survey your campus for leadership opportunities. Take advantage of training offered by student services, career counseling, and other staff. Many colleges sponsor peer-counseling or paraprofessional programs that provide training in a particular area, such as peer health education, for students who subsequently instruct other students in an outreach setting. One popular position that offers training and challenge is that of a residence hall assistant/advisor who works with students under various circumstances as a resource, model, supporter, and disciplinarian. Leadership positions are likely to instill valuable, transferable, life-long skills as they did for Gerardo in Case in Point 4.2.

Realize that leadership positions usually place you in the types of situations described by Baxter Magolda's post-college sample. As a leader you are expected to function independently, exercise authority over others, form and execute subjective decisions, collaborate, deal with ambiguous situations, and live with the certain knowledge that there are few clear solutions to many circumstances you encounter. Several schools offer leadership courses or a minor or major in leadership studies. Search your academic bulletin or schedule for the availability of credit-based leadership courses. A minor in leadership is an excellent support to your academic major, especially if you aspire to reach the higher levels of your intended career. Also take advantage of paid or unpaid

CASE IN POINT 4.2   From Student Leader to College Leader

When one of Gerardo's former instructors asked him 20 years after graduation about his most valuable college experiences, Gerardo quickly named two leadership positions. As president of the student government his senior year, one of his responsibilities included periodic meetings with the president's planning committee that included key faculty, staff, and administrators. During these meetings, he learned about college operations, budgets, interpersonal communication patterns, management issues, student clout, and the political intrigues inherent in any organization. Gerardo was also a resident assistant during his last two years of college. As an "RA," he practiced communication, crisis management, and supervision skills that formed a strong foundation for the clinical skills he subsequently developed in his graduate clinical psychology program. In his two leadership positions, Gerardo was positively reinforced by the status and responsibilities each position held and by the respect that others accorded him. Now, as the director of a substance abuse training program and faculty member in a large metropolitan community college, *Dr.* Gerardo is convinced his two undergraduate leadership positions, along with the support of a counselor who saw his potential, were turning points in his college education.

tutoring opportunities that many academic departments offer. Not only do they enable you to master a body of knowledge, but they also strengthen your communication skills in a teaching role. Employers and graduate schools pay very close attention to an applicant's leadership background because it reflects a set of capabilities (especially in communication, responsibility, and decision making) that are not directly reflected on a transcript.

YOUR OTHER LIFE

We have shown how the themes of the post-college independent and contextual knower can be applied to your academic and co-curricular activities. To what extent do they fit into other dimensions of your life, including your job? If your part- or full-time job includes situations where you collaborate, function independently, exercise authority, formulate decisions, and operate in an ambiguous environment, you may be advancing gradually to higher levels of knowing. Be critical and honest about the role of these themes in your work setting, however. Even a challenging part-time job, because it is part-time, does not immerse you in the situations faced by the full-time employees. Work responsibilities can vary tremendously, and it is easy to oversimplify the operation and the effects of the themes that seem to explain the graduates' advancement to complex knowing. Use the following checklist to *roughly estimate* the extent to which the themes operate in your working environment.

To what extent does my job involve

	Never		Sometimes		Often
the expectation that I function independently, with little supervision?	1	2	3	4	5
acquiring job-related information from others regularly?	1	2	3	4	5
discussing new ideas with co-workers regularly?	1	2	3	4	5
exercising authority over others or control over my tasks?	1	2	3	4	5
making subjective decisions in the absence of objective criteria?	1	2	3	4	5
working in an environment characterized by much uncertainty or ambiguity?	1	2	3	4	5

If your responses were mainly 1s and 2s, your job produces a paycheck, but it does not appear to facilitate cognitive growth. If you marked mainly 4s and 5s, your paycheck may be only one major benefit, i.e., it appears that you are being challenged cognitively. Interpret your responses cautiously because the themes abstracted from Baxter Magolda's interview data are at best general indicators that may explain students' progress towards higher levels of knowing. Their validity and reliability need to be established through more empirical research. Your responses may help you think about the kinds of challenge you enjoy and dislike in a job.

As citizens of a great democracy, we live in times when highly complex social and international issues affect our daily lives. What actions will bring about peace in the Middle East? To what extent can gay couples be effective parents? Is abortion simply an issue of right or wrong? Do the "three strikes and you're out" laws really work? Should the terminally ill exercise choice in their treatments? Your beliefs about such complex issues should not be formed through blind adherence to authorities, conformity with peers, watching headline news, or attending to only one side of the issue. Explore *multiple perspectives* and examine the *evidence* on both sides of the issues in their *particular contexts.* Television programs such as the evening PBS *News Hour With Jim Lehrer* and *Frontline,* ABC's *Nightline,* and the Sunday morning network news programs typically present contrasting positions on major issues. National Public Radio (NPR) devotes substantial time to specific issues. Programs where the primary focus is on a domineering anchor and not the news itself may tell you more about the person than the news.

Although several programs examine controversial issues, recognize that some news anchors are biased. Be willing to study an issue using many sources, written and electronic. In a 1993 commencement speech, the late astronomer Carl Sagan advised, "Equip yourself with a baloney-detection kit. Because there is an enormous amount of baloney that has to be winnowed out before the few shining gems of truth and reality can be glimpsed" (Bryant 2003). Be willing to take a position and argue it, and be open to modifying your position when new evidence is presented. Try to establish and articulate your convictions. Getting involved takes time, effort, honesty, and resilience. Few people have time to investigate all the major issues in depth, but if AIDS, world hunger, the slave trade of women and children, lax DUI laws, war in the Mideast, or similar problems tap into your interests and convictions, pursue them. The first job or career of many new graduates is often anchored to the social issues they pursued as college students.

Finally, our relationships with family, friends, and significant others are regular occasions to listen and weigh contrasting views, defend and reevaluate our convictions, act responsibly, collaborate, and deal with uncertainties. In short, we do not have to wait until our first job to view the world as a contextual knower. We can take steps now to advance our assumptions about knowing. Are you willing to take the risk? To expend the efforts? To face the uncertainties? To change your views? English writer James Allen remarked, "To live is to think and act, and to think and act is to change."

KNOWING AND THE BIG PICTURE

Baxter Magolda's amazing longitudinal study shows that college students travel through four progressively more complex stages in their epistemological development, stages that differ in dependence on authorities and the management of uncertainty. The stages do not match a college's four academic milestones. Studies show that most students graduate as transitional knowers (Baxter Magolda 1992, King and Kitchener 1994). The complex assumptions of knowing rapidly increase after college, however, when individuals directly experience what they learn, function independently, collaborate, exercise authority, and execute decisions in ambiguous situations. We encourage you to welcome assignments (Welcome? at least be open to them!) that generate multiple perspectives, call on your experiences, form and defend your convictions, and collaborate with peers. Study abroad, travel, service-learning projects, internships, and other forms of experiential learning are excellent opportunities for immersion in other cultures or subcultures. Get involved in the co-curriculum, especially in progressively more responsible leadership roles where you can develop lifelong and marketable skills that challenge your existing assumptions about the world. Our personal lives, jobs, and identity as citizens are also rich sources for nurturing cognitive development.

ARE *YOU* THINKING?

While reading this material, have you asked yourself if there is evidence to support the suggestions being introduced? If "yes," congratulate yourself for thinking critically. In their review of research conducted on the relationship between cognitive development and students' out-of-class experiences, Terenzini, Pascarella, and Blimling (1996) reported positive effects of student-faculty interactions, study abroad, and internships on cognitive development and learning. Students' interactions with peers, faculty, and staff seem to be the most powerful influence on students. Extracurricular activities and living in a residence hall seem to have indirect and cumulative effects on development. To the extent that residence hall life is designed to integrate academic and social dimensions, it too can promote cognitive development.

While reading this material, have you asked yourself if other researchers reached similar conclusions? If so, your contextual-level questioning is praise-worthy. Baxter Magolda's findings generally support the work of her predecessors, including Perry (1981), Belenky, Clinchy, Goldberger, and Tarule (1986), and King and Kitchener (1994), who used similar models of knowing. Have you questioned the extent to which her findings can be generalized to other groups? Again, your question reveals contextual-level thinking. In fact, Baxter Magolda's sample was predominantly midwestern, white, middle-class, younger students (the dynamics of the context in which the study was conducted). Before you close the book in frustration because you do not fit into one or more of these categories, remember from your previous science classes how complexities and uncertainties characterize research. We have no reason to believe that her findings cannot be generalized to similar groups of college students. What if you are over 30 years old? Does this mean you are already a contextual knower (another good question about contexts!)? Not necessarily. Growth in cognitive complexity has more to do with the quality of one's past experience than age alone. Have you traveled widely? Read challenging books? Successfully managed serious personal challenges? Been active in community events? Learned about cultures and history? Kept up with current events? Worked in challenging jobs? If "yes," chances are good that the assumptions you hold about your world are more advanced than other students. However, if too much time is spent in front of mind-deadening electronic media or if your intellectual life is seldom challenged, age alone does not automatically admit you to the contextual-knower club. Nor does reading *about* cognitive development (as you have been doing) accelerate it. In the words of the anonymous quotation that began this chapter, "education is the process of *moving* from cocksure ignorance to thoughtful uncertainty." We hope this chapter has stimulated you to move toward thoughtful uncertainty.

To conclude, (1) knowing about how you know (the four stages), (2) knowing that most students do not reach epistemological maturity until after graduation, and (most important), (3) knowing what to do during college to prepare for your future should reduce some of your uncertainties. But we are not certain that it will! How will you handle this uncertainty?

JOURNAL STARTERS

1. (a) Briefly describe two or three important beliefs (about anything) that you hold with great certainty and conviction. What conditions or events have caused you to maintain certainty about these beliefs? (b) Briefly describe two or three important beliefs, which, over the years, have

become much less certain for you. What events or factors caused you to be less certain about them?

2. Review the section "What Can You Do with this Information?" Then describe two things you would like to do, realistically, in the near future to move toward a higher level of cognitive growth. Write yourself a plan for accomplishing each task and attach it to your mirror or refrigerator. For example, if you are interested in a service learning project or study abroad, write down the name of the office or contact person, its location, and when you will make contact.

3. Describe two or three of the most significant ideas or insights you gained from reading this chapter. What are some of the concerns, questions, or criticisms you have about the material discussed above?

REFERENCES

Astin, A. W. (1999). Involvement in learning revisited: Lessons we have learned. *Journal of College Student Development,* 40(5): 587–598.

Baxter Magolda, M. B. (1992). *Knowing and reasoning in students: Gender-related patterns in students' intellectual development.* San Francisco, CA: Jossey-Bass.

Baxter Magolda, M. B. (1994). Post-college experiences and epistemology. *The Review of Higher Education.* 18(1): 25–44.

Baxter Magolda, M. B. (1996). Epistemological development in graduate and professional education. *The Review of Higher Education.* 19(3): 283–304.

Belenky, M. F., Clinchy, B. M., Goldberger, N. R., and Tarule, J. M. (1997). *Women's ways of knowing.* Tenth Anniversary Edition. New York: Basic Books.

Bryant, A. (2003). Now, before we commence. *How to get into college: 2004 Edition.* p. 72. New York: Newsweek, Inc. and Kaplan, Inc.

Hettich, P. (1998). *Learning skills for college and career.* Pacific Grove, CA: Brooks/Cole.

King, P. M. and Kitchener, K. S. (1994). *Developing reflective judgment: Understanding and promoting intellectual growth and critical thinking in adolescents and adults.* San Francisco, CA: Jossey-Bass.

Perry, W. G. (1981). Cognitive and ethical growth: The making of meaning. In *The modern American college.* A. W. Chickering and Associates, 76–116. San Francisco, CA: Jossey-Bass.

Terenzini, P. T., Pascarella, E. T., Blimling. G. S. (1996). Students' out-of-class experiences and their influence on learning and cognitive development: A literature review. *Journal of College Student Learning.* 40(5): 610–623.

5

Intelligence Revisited

What It Really Means
to Be Smart

As an elementary-school student, I failed miserably on the IQ tests I had
to take. I was incredibly test-anxious. Just the sight of the school
psychologist coming into the classroom to give a group IQ test
sent me into a wild panic attack.

ROBERT J. STERNBERG

Because of his low test scores, Robert Sternberg and his teachers thought
he might be "dumb." Thanks to a fourth grade teacher who believed
that he could do better, Robert worked harder, exceeded everyone's
expectations, and quickly became an "A" student (Sternberg 1996). His early
school experiences must have "burned" themselves into his memory, for
Robert J. Sternberg is one of today's most productive and respected cognitive
psychologists. His theory of Successful Intelligence is summarized in the following section.

In chapter 2 you learned that years of educational conditioning create certain beliefs, expectations, and habits regarding work, life, and success. The
Kaplan/*Newsweek* annual edition of *How to Get Into College: 2004 Edition*
reports, "Colleges are putting more weight than ever on standardized tests.
Next to grades, they're the most important factor that admissions committees
use to sift through the pile" (Stern 2003, p. 46). The emphasis on test scores is
reinforced later in college during the stressful ordeal of applying to graduate
or professional school. Terms such as GRE, GMAT, LSAT, and MCAT may
provoke in you a level of anxiety matched only by the sight of flashing red

lights in your rearview mirror. Students with the highest test scores are rewarded with scholarships and entry to the best schools, although other factors are also important. Their achievements *are* commendable. You respect, sometimes grudgingly, the academic accomplishments of the Merit Scholar and the "A" student. However, you have been in college long enough to know that grades do not necessarily reflect learning, because learning is intangible. It is inferred and measured indirectly through its manifestations in papers, projects, and (of course) exams. We do not wish to debate the merits and pitfalls of tests; like them or not, they are a dominating symbol of an American college education. Yet the understandable but unfortunate perception that grades and standardized test scores are the primary ingredient of intelligence complicates the transition from college to career. Too many people believe that high grades are associated with rapid success in the workplace (sometimes they are) and that low grades predict failure (usually, they do not). The purpose of this chapter is to introduce you to several perspectives on what it means to be intelligent so that you do not cross the graduation stage believing that your intelligence is wrapped up in your GPA, whatever it might be. Had young Robert Sternberg acted on his early beliefs that poor tests scores signify inferior intelligence, it is highly unlikely that he would have become a major force in any field, especially cognitive psychology.

SO WHAT IS INTELLIGENCE?

Experts still do not agree (it seems they never do!) about the nature of intelligence, so we exempt you from a scholarly discussion of this topic. Early researcher Charles Spearman claimed that a general ability (the "g" factor) underlies all forms of intelligent behavior, although people manifest separate abilities. In contrast, contemporary scholar Howard Gardner believes that we have eight multiple intelligences, including linguistic, logical-mathematical, spatial, musical, bodily-kinesthetic, naturalistic, interpersonal, and intrapersonal (Sternberg 1999). The last two forms are key concepts throughout this book, including this chapter.

NOTHING SUCCEEDS LIKE
SUCCESSFUL INTELLIGENCE

Sternberg agrees conceptually with the multiple intelligence theory because behavior is far too complex to be accounted for by a general factor or by the types of IQ tests that induced his panic. His theory of Successful Intelligence consists of four elements that expand traditional notions (Sternberg 1999).

"*Element 1*: Intelligence is defined in terms of the ability to achieve success in life in terms of one's personal standards, within one's sociocultural context" (p. 296). According to this view, what makes behavior intelligent is relative, in part, to one's choices within his or her social environment. For example, who is more successful—the wealthy physician whose office is located on Chicago's Magnificent Mile or the undercompensated but socially concerned physician working in rural Mississippi? Who is more successful—the "B−" student who works 25 hours a week, sustains solid friendships, and participates in school activities or the "A+" student whose sole activity is studying and attending classes? (Note: By this definition, successful criminals could be viewed as intelligent, and many are, but we can only condemn their form of "success.")

"*Element 2*: One's ability to achieve success depends on one's capitalizing on one's strengths and correcting or compensating for one's weaknesses." (p. 297). Sternberg observes that traditional tests of intelligence specify various fixed sets of abilities, but the reality is that people achieve success in different ways even within a particular occupation. Let's say, for instance, that you are an extroverted individual who likes to travel, enjoys working with people, and possesses good organizational and managerial skills. You want to enter the aviation field to become a commercial airline pilot, but you lack the physical qualifications to fly. Is there no future for you in aviation? You could enjoy a satisfying career in an aviation administration position that enables you to further develop your skills and personal traits and still travel. In other words, "know thyself" is an excellent prescription for acting intelligently.

"*Element 3*: Success is attained through a balance of analytical, creative and practical abilities." (p. 297). Sternberg's third element is so important to expanding your concept of intelligence that we will elaborate. *Analytical abilities* include reasoning, problem solving, analysis, evaluation, and judgment—major focuses in most college courses. Yet success in life and work requires other forms of thinking.

> Analytical thinking is required to solve problems and to judge the quality of ideas. Creative intelligence is required to formulate good problems and ideas in the first place. Practical intelligence is needed to use the ideas and their analysis in an effective way in one's everyday life (Sternberg 1996, pp. 127–128).

Creative intelligence includes the ability to produce novel ideas or products, to think innovatively and insightfully, and to connect or combine ideas in unusual but valued ways. Depending on the nature of course material and the instructor, creative thinking is a part of all academic disciplines that should be reflected in your courses. An instructor may not use the term *creativity*, but assignments that require writing, problem solving, project design, generating ideas, or hypothesis testing tap your creative intelligence. Thinking creatively is not a passive process for, as Thomas Edison observed, "Genius is one percent inspiration and ninety-nine percent perspiration."

Sternberg views *practical intelligence* as common sense, i.e., knowing what to do and how to do it when the situations arise. Practical intelligence depends on tacit knowledge, essentially the knowledge "one needs to know to work effectively in an environment that one is not explicitly taught and that often is not even verbalized" (Sternberg 1999, p. 305). Much of what we know and do in a particular situation is based on our tacit knowledge. For example, when your decision to enroll late for the new academic term forces you into a course taught by the infamous Dr. Curmudgeon, your practical intelligence guides your decision either to remain in the course and adapt to its demands, attempt to change the professor's behavior (Good luck!), or somehow to find a substitute course. Your tacit knowledge about your likely success in each option is derived from your experiences as a student, and it guides your decision. The tacit knowledge we accumulate through daily living contributes tremendously to the practical intelligence (or lack of it) we display every day in the numerous decisions we make—the clothes we put on, the alternate route to work chosen during road repairs, our response to a supervisor's request for feedback, and the manner in which we participate in a group discussion.

Recall the studies about workplace preparation from chapter 2. Graduates believed they were well prepared in knowledge and skills acquired in their major (a predominance of analytical thinking), but they were less prepared to apply their knowledge to work contexts (Gardner 1998), *where creative and practical intelligence* is needed. Analytic thinking enables you to master abstract concepts and explain them on an exam, but *using* the concepts to formulate or solve problems in a practical situation demands creative and practical forms of thinking that may not be encountered in coursework. This is *not* to devalue analytic thinking. On the contrary, skills in analysis, reasoning, problem solving, and critical thinking are absolutely essential, but they are insufficient for the complex personal and professional situations you will encounter that require "thinking outside the box." Different situations often require different ways of thinking that are not acquired in many college classrooms.

"*Element 4*: Balancing of abilities is achieved to adapt to, shape, and select environments" (Sternberg 1999, p. 298). Two important ideas are embedded in this brief statement. First, a balance among analytical, creative, and practical forms of intelligence is essential. Recall the example that compared the "A+" student who only studied and attended classes with the "B−" student who also worked and maintained a social life. Chances are that the "A+" student has highly developed analytical and, possibly, creative intelligence, but practical intelligence is likely deficient, given the lack of social interaction and the student's narrow focus on academics. Chances are the "B−" student possesses a better *balance* of analytical, creative, and practical intelligence, given the breadth of involvement. Furthermore, knowing when and how to use your abilities is more important than simply possessing them (Sternberg 1996). As one teacher frequently said to talented underachievers, "There's nothing so wasteful as unused potential."

Secondly, adapting to a particular environment is often a passive process, whereas creating or selecting your environments (including work, living, and personal relationships) requires initiative, persistence, and a proactive attitude. Recall Baxter Magolda's claim in chapter 4 that active involvement promotes higher levels of knowing. In short, intelligent persons do not wait for an opportunity to come to them; they seek the opportunity. As a junior or senior, you know that your college education must be *achieved,* not received.

In summary, Sternberg's theory of successful intelligence explodes the myth that intelligence is best reflected in test scores, grades, and GPAs. His ideas can liberate you from narrow and often negative self-images created in the past regarding your intelligence (e.g., "I've never been good at . . ."). Being smart really means to achieve success in terms of (a) your standards within your sociocultural context; (b) acting with a clear knowledge of your strengths and weaknesses; (c) establishing a balance among your analytic, creative, and practical abilities; and (d) knowing when to adapt to, shape, and select your environments. It would be a challenge to reduce this perspective on intelligence to a letter grade or test score!

EMOTIONAL INTELLIGENCE

The term, *emotional intelligence,* is an oxymoron to people who think of intelligence primarily as logic, analysis, and objective, calculated reasoning. (Remember that Mr. Spock and the Terminator *are* fictional characters.). On the other hand, you may believe in "listening to your heart" and tuning in to "your gut-level feeling." The term, *emotional intelligence,* originated in the 1990s and, predictably, generated considerable excitement and controversy. Below is one widely accepted definition.

> Emotional intelligence refers to an ability to recognize the meanings of emotions and their relationships, and to reason and problem-solve on the basis of them. Emotional intelligence is involved in the capacity to perceive emotions, assimilate emotion-related feelings, understand the information of those emotions, and manage them (Mayer, Caruso, and Salovey 1999, p. 267).

Included in this definition are three primary but interrelated abilities of EI (emotional intelligence):

- the ability to accurately perceive and recognize our own and others' emotions;
- the ability to understand emotions, including knowing how emotions unfold and how to reason about them, sometimes called "emotional script;" and
- the ability to manage and regulate emotions effectively. (Ciarrochi, Forgas, and Mayer 2001). (You may recall from chapter 3 that managing emotions is vector two in the Chickering and Reisser theory of psychosocial development.)

You learned in school about reading, writing, " 'rithmitic," and reasoning, but when did you learn how to perceive, recognize, and understand your emotions? Was there a course on "emotion management" that you missed, or is EI developed only through painful trial-and-error behavior as you mature? In a discussion that relates EI to self-actualization, Ciarrochi et al. (2001) list ten key emotional, personal, and social abilities that comprise the structure of emotional intelligence.

- *Self-regard:* The ability to accurately perceive and appraise ourselves
- *Emotional self-awareness:* The ability to be aware of and understand our emotions
- *Assertiveness:* The ability to constructively express our emotions and ourselves
- *Stress tolerance:* The ability to effectively manage our emotions
- *Impulse control:* The ability to control our emotions
- *Reality testing:* The ability to objectively validate our feelings and thoughts
- *Flexibility:* The ability to adapt and adjust our feelings and thoughts to new situations
- *Problem solving:* The ability to solve our personal and interpersonal problems
- *Empathy:* The ability to be aware of and understand others' emotions
- *Interpersonal relationship:* The ability to relate well with others (p. 87)

Pause for a few minutes and recall one or two of the numerous occasions during the past 24 hours when you exhibited your emotional intelligence. What specific EI abilities were involved, whether expressed appropriately or inappropriately? The events could have occurred with a friend, family member, teacher, supervisor, acquaintance, or when you were alone with your thoughts. As EI sometimes manifests itself in subtle ways, try to recall as many details as possible about the event before you respond. Use a separate sheet or sketch the occasion in the space below. For example, on the left side, identify the occasion in a few words. In the middle of your sheet, enter the key personal and social abilities involved. On the right side, note your general level of satisfaction with the event by marking a plus ($+$) if you are satisfied, a minus ($-$) if you are dissatisfied, or a check mark ($\checkmark$) if you are neither satisfied nor dissatisfied. Finally, note any changes you would make if you could repeat the event.

Event	EI Abilities Involved	Satisfaction	Changes

Based on your analysis of these situations, to what extent is it reasonable to say that our ability to perceive, understand, and regulate our emotions is one way to demonstrate our intelligence?

Often our judgments of others are based on the ways they use their emotions to resolve problems. Case in Point 5.1 illustrates contrasting examples in which two students dealt with low grades.

CASE IN POINT 5.1   Dealing With "Ds"

Jessica held down a full-time job while enrolled as a full-time student, with responsibilities at home for two much younger siblings. She was average-to-above-average in her analytical abilities. Her grades were often below average, and on more than one occasion she received a "D" in courses that required a "C−" or higher. Typically she complained to her instructors about her grades and expected teachers to be lenient because of her personal circumstances. Jessica had to repeat a few courses in which she received a "D." Her advisor discouraged Jessica from taking a full course load while working full-time, but she continued her dual commitments even though she could have attended college on a part-time basis.

One time after she received a "D" grade, she left a voice-mail message that accused her instructor of being unfair and unsympathetic to students. The instructor invited Jessica to meet and discuss her scores on the various assignments, but she refused and subsequently told classmates how unfair the teacher was. Because Jessica had acted this way with other teachers on similar occasions and refused to accept responsibility for her own decisions, no one sympathized with her. Nevertheless, she continued to complain about the bad treatment, refused to reduce her course load, finished her final term with barely a 2.0 GPA, and was forced to enroll in another academic term to obtain her degree.

Review the list of 10 abilities that comprise EI. Then identify as best you can (given the limited information and the knowledge that EI is only one perspective for understanding behavior) those EI abilities that represent deficiencies and strengths in Jessica's approach to solving her problems.

Strengths	Weaknesses

Joshua was a full-time student who worked part-time at the library. He found it hard to master abstract concepts, especially in courses that were theory-oriented. His essay exam answers and the questions he asked in class generally reflected a very concrete level of thinking and a poor understanding of course material. He worked inconsistently in a math course required for the major, seldom met with the course tutor, and received a final grade of "D." He willingly re-enrolled in the course and saw the tutor more often, but received a "D" again. During Joshua's junior year, his advisor encouraged him to switch to a particular major that had fewer quantitative requirements. Joshua elected not to change to the new major even though he had completed several of its courses. He continued to receive "Ds", felt frustrated with his situation, and discussed it calmly with his advisor.

When encouraged to visit the director of the university's learning disabilities program and the university counseling office, he willingly followed through. He tested negative for a learning disability and attended a few counseling sessions for personal issues. Each time Joshua met with his teachers and advisor, he understood his situation, accepted responsibility for his decisions, and communicated calmly. As Joshua approached graduation, he still needed to complete two major requirements, including the math course (which the department chair could not waive). He was encouraged to complete the course in another department or another college.

(Continued)

CASE IN POINT 5.1　Continued

Joshua's teachers and advisor were not convinced that he had done his best, yet they felt bad that he had not succeeded. They appreciated the manner in which he interacted with them during their many meetings.

Review the list of EI abilities for Joshua as you did for Jessica (with the same constraints) and identify those strengths and deficiencies in Joshua's behavior.

Strengths　　　　Weaknesses

_____

_____

_____

The information provided does not justify a detailed analysis of how each student manifested emotional intelligence, but we offer a few cautious observations. Jessica and Joshua each made decisions about their coursework and academic majors that led to frustration and failure to complete requirements in a timely manner.

In general, each student displayed problems with self-regard (over-estimating their capacity to complete academic requirements), problem solving, reality testing, and flexibility. Jessica was aggressive (versus assertive) and blamed her teachers for her low grades. Joshua did not act impulsively or express anger at his teachers, but we don't know if he directed anger in other ways (e.g., to himself). He maintained a healthy interpersonal relationship with his teachers, whereas Jessica alienated hers. If you were at a social gathering with Jessica and Joshua, with whom would you prefer to talk? Why? If Joshua or Jessica were a co-worker, with whom would you prefer to work? Why? Be sure to read Journal Starter # 2 for opportunity to apply the EI abilities to someone you know.

EI in the Workplace and Beyond

How many people do you know who are unhappy with their jobs in spite of their analytic intelligence, technical skills, or job security? To what extent could the dissatisfaction reside in their emotional skills or those of others? Emotional intelligence is an important factor in hiring and evaluating employees, and Ciarrochi et al. (2001) recommend that it play a role in career development, training, coaching, and leadership training. They conclude

> *Identifying* [italics added] emotions provides awareness of emotions and the ability to read accurately other people's emotions. *Using* emotions provides a means to generate ideas, a feeling, or a team spirit. *Understanding* emotions offers insights into what motivates people and others' points of view. Finally, *managing* emotions allows you to stay open to your feelings, which contain valuable information, and use them constructively. (p 164)

In *Working With Emotional Intelligence,* Daniel Goleman (1998) reports on the application of EI in corporate settings. Although he differs with researchers such as Ciarrochi et al. in the definition and classification of EI skills, Goleman emphasizes the importance of EI in personnel recruitment, training, team development, influence/power, communication, conflict man-agement, and leadership issues. One graduating senior who learned about EI

CASE IN POINT 5.2   Customer Service at the Photo Counter

Kim took several negatives from an important family event in carefully marked envelopes to the local drug store photo counter to have reprints made using sale-price coupons. Kim wanted five copies each of eight negatives (each from a different strip), one copy each of five negatives (from the same strip), and three 5" x 7" enlargements from still another negative—all for the sale price of about $18. Because the order was relatively complex, Kim planned to transfer the information about the 14 negatives to the official store envelopes, but the clerk abruptly insisted on doing it herself. When Kim picked up the order the next day, the same sales clerk charged the regular price of $30 for the reprint order. When Kim pointed out the overcharge, the clerk recalculated the costs and corrected the charge, but did not apologize for the $12 error.

After returning home Kim discovered several mistakes in the order: One enlargement was missing; there were four (not five) copies of some prints; Kim was overcharged for five prints in the original estimate, and one negative was erroneously reprinted (Kim's mistake). Kim returned to the store the next day and explained the mistakes (the store's and Kim's) to another clerk on duty. The clerk processed the changes, filled out a refund form, and asked the manager to approve it. At no time did any of the three store personnel involved acknowledge or apologize for the errors and inconvenience caused by their mistakes. Throughout the various interactions with store personnel, Kim did not openly criticize them but pointed out the errors calmly. Kim concluded that the quality and price of the reprints were good, but customer service "stunk."

Review the list of 10 abilities that comprise EI and identify those that

- store personnel failed to demonstrate when relating to Kim
- store personnel failed to see in themselves
- Kim demonstrated or failed to demonstrate, if applicable

Whether you work in retail sales, wait on tables, or serve people in other ways, a primary principle of customer service is to put yourself in the customer's shoes (i.e., show *empathy*). None of the employees seemed capable of, or felt like, identifying with Kim's frustration. *Interpersonal relationships* with this customer was unimportant. Chances are Kim's future photo needs will be handled at a different store.

William Bridges (1994) emphasizes that in today's world of work employees must recognize at all times that they serve two customers, the *internal customer* (members of your organization that provides your job and salary) and the *external customer* who supplies the money that makes your job and salary possible. To serve those customers well, employees must demonstrate the emotional and social abilities that comprise emotional intelligence.

---

in class returned from a job interview with a nationally known computer sales organization and reported excitedly that most questions during the group interview focused on issues and situations relating to EI abilities. We believe that her experience is not unusual. Part-time jobs, especially those involving customer contact, are excellent opportunities for observing EI in action, as Case in Point 5.2 attests.

By now you are waiting impatiently to learn how you can increase your EI. Ciarrochi et al. devote less than two pages to this topic. Other investigators are similarly cautious because research does not yet support claims for strengthening EI beyond the following statements. You do not have to search the "pop-psych" shelves long to find prescriptions for increasing your EI IQ, but the social scientists who study EI are cautious in their recommendations:

- Learn to read people's emotions by attending to emotional cues, reading between the lines, and attending to facial expressions as well as verbal expressions.

- Generate emotions in yourself (using techniques such as visualization, imagery, breathing, and muscle relaxation) to create positive moods for relaxation or for energizing others.

- Learn to manage emotions by becoming aware of them and subsequently using them to solve a problem.

Having knowledge about EI may not increase your emotional intelligence, but when you monitor your behavior in situations requiring it, you take an important first step to strengthening the three abilities listed above—recognizing, understanding, and regulating emotions. Pay close attention to how you interact with teachers, classmates, family members, supervisors, and friends, whether you are in quiet or tense situations. Monitor how you think and behave in class, lab, group projects, at work, in the cafeteria, at home, and in your personal relationships. Give yourself honest feedback and seek it from those whom you respect and trust. Think smart, pay close attention, listen, reflect, obtain feedback, and change what you must when you must change it. To help you understand more about the concept of EI, complete the scale contained in Case in Point 5.3.

THE COMPETENCE PERSPECTIVE

Successful intelligence and emotional intelligence are psychological perspectives on what it means to be smart. How else is intelligence viewed in the workplace? Employers prefer to use such terms as *competences, competencies,* or *skills* to describe specific (often measurable) work-related abilities that reflect intelligent behaviors to which standards for performance can be applied. For example, in *Recruiting Trends: 2002–2003,* the Career Services and Placement/ Collegiate Employment Research Institute (2002) summarizes the results of a survey conducted of 376 employers nationwide who represent the manufacturing and professional services sector. When asked to identify the five most important competencies or skills a college candidate must possess to be *considered* for employment, employers responded (in order of frequency):

- Communication skills: solid abilities in verbal, written, listening, and presentation (i.e., the ability to respond to questions and critiques of presentational material)

CASE IN POINT 5.3   Assessing Your Emotional I.Q.

You may develop a sense of your "emotional IQ" by completing the following scale.

Instructions: Using a scale of 1 through 4, where 1 = strongly disagree, 2 = somewhat disagree, 3 = somewhat agree, and 4 = strongly agree, respond to the following statements.

_____ 1. I know when to speak about my personal problems to others.

_____ 2. When I am faced with obstacles, I remember times I faced similar obstacles and overcame them.

_____ 3. I expect that I will do well on most things.

_____ 4. Other people find it easy to confide in me.

_____ 5. I find it easy to understand the nonverbal messages of other people.

_____ 6. Some of the major events of my life have led me to reevaluate what is important and not important.

_____ 7. When my mood changes, I see new possibilities.

_____ 8. Emotions are one of the things that make life worth living.

_____ 9. I am aware of my emotions as I experience them.

_____ 10. I expect good things to happen to me.

_____ 11. I like to share my emotions with other people.

_____ 12. When I experience a positive emotion, I know how to make it last.

_____ 13. I arrange events others enjoy.

_____ 14. I seek out activities that make me happy.

_____ 15. I am aware of the nonverbal messages I send to others.

_____ 16. I present myself in a way that makes a good impression on others.

_____ 17. When I am in a positive mood, solving problems is easy for me.

_____ 18. By looking at facial expressions, I can recognize the emotions that others are feeling.

_____ 19. I know why my emotions change.

_____ 20. When I am in a positive mood, I am able to come up with new ideas.

_____ 21. I have control over my emotions.

_____ 22. I easily recognize my emotions as I experience them.

_____ 23. I motivate myself by imagining a good outcome to the tasks I do.

_____ 24. I compliment others when they have done something well.

_____ 25. I am aware of the nonverbal message other people send.

_____ 26. When another person tells me about an important event in their life, I almost feel as though I have experienced this event myself.

_____ 27. When I feel a change in emotions, I tend to come up with new ideas.

_____ 28. When I am faced with a challenge, I usually rise to the occasion.

(Continued)

CASE IN POINT 5.3 Continued

_____ 29. I know what other people are feeling just by looking at them.

_____ 30. I help other people feel better when they are down.

_____ 31. I use good moods to help myself keep trying in the face of obstacles.

_____ 32. I can tell how people are feeling by listening to the tone of their voices.

Scoring:

Add your responses to questions 1, 6, 7, 8, 12, 14, 17, 19, 20, 22, 23, and 27. Put this total here _____. This is your *self-awareness* score.

Add your responses to questions, 4, 15, 18, 25, 29, and 32. Put this total here _____. This is your *social awareness* score.

Add your responses to questions 2, 3, 9, 10, 16, 21, 28, and 31. Put this total here _____. This is your *self-management* score.

Add your responses to questions 5, 11, 13, 24, 26, and 30. Put this total here _____. This is your *social skills* score.

According to Goleman, the higher your score in each of these four areas, the more emotionally intelligent you

are. People who score high (greater than 36) in *self-awareness* recognize their emotions and their effects on others, accurately assess their strengths and limitations, and have a strong sense of their self-worth and capabilities. People who score high (greater than 18) in *social awareness* are good at understanding others, taking an active interest in their concerns and and empathizing with them, and recognize the needs others have at work. People who score high (greater than 24) in *self-management* can keep their disruptive emotions and impulses under control, maintain standards of integrity and honesty, are conscientious, adapt their behaviors to changing situations, and have internal standards of excellence that guide their behaviors. People who have high (greater than 18) *social skills* sense others' developmental needs, inspire and lead groups, and send clear and convincing messages, build effective interpersonal relationships, and work well with others to achieve shared goals.

SOURCE: Reprinted From *Personality and Individual Differences*, Vol. 25, 1998, pp. 167–177, Schutte et al, "Development and validation of a measure of emotional intelligence." Copyright 1998. With permission from Elsevier.

- Computer/technical aptitudes (with expectations increasing for higher knowledge and skills)

- Leadership: ability to take charge or relinquish control; management abilities

- Interpersonal abilities: skills in relating to and inspiring others to participate or reduce conflict among coworkers

- Teamwork: working collaboratively with others while maintaining control over autonomous assignments

The report adds that these competencies should be shaped by a combination of personal traits that reflect initiative, motivation, adaptability, a work ethic (hard work and dependability), honesty, integrity, the ability to plan and organize multiple tasks, and ability to provide a "customer service" orientation to one's work. (Recall the role customer service played in the Case in Point 5.2 case study.) The applicant also needs to bring the following skills or experiences that "bind" or hold together these characteristics into a "total package": critical thinking/problem solving; intelligence and common sense; willingness to learn quickly and continuously; and work-related experiences. *Recruiting Trends 2002–2003* concluded its annual survey with this harsh dose of reality:

> Because the economy is moving so quickly, candidates must enter their position already demonstrating their command of these competencies. There is neither time nor luxury of training a highly qualified academic candidate in these skills. Employers demand that the "total package" be delivered at graduation (p. 33).

In other words, changes in the economy and in the nature of work have pushed responsibilities down the employee hierarchy to the point where college graduates are now expected to enter employment with competencies at a much higher level than would have been required one or two decades ago.

The results of such surveys often generate debate in academic circles regarding the role of education versus training. Critics argue that college should prepare its graduates for life, not merely for careers; that liberal arts courses are necessary to develop a person's knowledge of the world, appreciation of cultures, personal growth, and ethical and critical thinking; and that graduates should be generalists, not specialists. Some educators disagree on the last point.

> The debate as to whether college graduates should be specialists or generalists is over; they need to be both. Today's college graduates need to possess specialized knowledge and skills plus general skills that will provide them with the ability to adapt to whatever changes come next. It is simply not good enough to be able to access information. Graduates must be able to apply the information to solve problems (Evers, Rush, and Berdrow 1998. p. 3).

Evers and his associates conducted a longitudinal study of advanced college students, graduates (from recent to several years out), and graduates' managers to determine which competencies and skills are deemed most important in the work place. The researchers deliberately omitted technical and quantitative skills due to constraints imposed by the scope of the study. (You must remember, however, that computer/technical aptitudes was the second most frequently mentioned skill set in the *Recruiting Trends* survey above; continuous improvement is essential.) Using data collected over a two year period from the three groups of participants, they applied a statistical procedure (factor analysis) that reduced the ratings of 18 competencies and skills into four groups that they labeled the *bases of competence* shown in Table 5.1.

Table 5.1 The Bases of Competence

Communicating

- Interpersonal: involves working well with others, understanding their needs, and being sympathetic with them
- Listening: involves being attentive when others are speaking and responding effectively to others' comments during conversation
- Oral Communication: involves the ability to present information verbally to others, either one-to-one or in groups
- Written Communication: involves the effective writing of formal reports and business correspondence, as well as informal notes and memos

Managing Self

- Learning: involves the ability to gain knowledge from everyday experiences and formal education experiences
- Personal Organization/Time Management: involves managing several tasks at once, being able to set priorities and allocate time efficiently in order to meet deadlines
- Personal Strengths: comprises maintaining a high energy level; motivating oneself to function at optimal levels of performance; functioning in stressful situations; maintaining a positive attitude; working independently; and responding appropriately to constructive criticism
- Problem Solving/Analytic: consists of identifying, prioritizing, and solving problems—individually or in groups. Includes the ability to ask the right questions, sort out the many facets of a problem, and contribute ideas as well as answers regarding the problem

Managing People and Tasks

- Coordinating: involves being able to coordinate the work of others and encourage positive group relationships
- Decision Making: involves making timely decisions on the basis of a thorough assessment of the short- and long-term effects of decisions, recognizing the political and ethical implications, and being able to identify those who will be affected by the decisions made
- Leadership/Influence: involves the ability to give direction and guidance to others and to delegate work tasks to others in a manner that proves to be effective and motivates others to do their best
- Managing Conflict: involves the ability to identify sources of conflict between oneself and others, or among other people, and to take steps to overcome disharmony
- Planning and Organizing: involves being able to determine the tasks to be carried out toward meeting objectives, perhaps assigning some of the tasks to others, monitoring the progress made against the plan, and revising a plan to include new information

Mobilizing Innovation and Change

- Ability to Conceptualize: involves the ability to combine relevant information from a number of sources, to integrate information into more general contexts, and to apply information to new or broader contexts
- Creativity/Innovation/Change: involves the ability to adapt to situations of change, at times initiating change and providing 'novel' solutions to problems
- Risk Taking: involves taking reasonable risks by recognizing alternative or different ways of meeting objectives, while at the same time recognizing the potential negative outcomes and monitoring the progress toward the set of objectives
- Visioning: involves the ability to conceptualize the future of the organization or group and provide innovative paths for the organization or group to follow

SOURCES: From *The Bases of Competence: Skills for Lifelong Learning and Employability* by F. T. Evers, J. C. Rush and I. Berdrow. 1998. San Francisco, CA: Jossey-Bass. This material is by permission of John Wiley and Sons, Inc.

Do not feel overwhelmed by what you have just read! Probably, few students graduate highly skilled in all 18 competencies. When survey participants were queried about competencies at which they were most proficient, it should not surprise you to learn that communicating and managing self received the highest ratings. Success in college depends substantially on the degree to which you master these eight skills and, at least some skills in the managing people and tasks and mobilizing innovation and change. In fact, Hettich (1998) distinguishes college's overt curriculum (coursework in the academic disciplines) from its equally important covert curriculum (routine skill-related activities, behaviors, and attitudes transacted inside and outside the classroom that reflect a student's overall work orientation).

When graduates were asked which of the 18 skills are most important to develop, they indicated (in order of importance): leadership, creativity, managing conflict, and time management. When the managers of these graduates were asked the same question, they responded: leadership, managing conflict, visioning, and risk taking.

As you study the 18 skills that form the bases of competence, it is apparent that college affords students opportunities to become liberally educated while developing general and special work-related skills. Your challenge is to recognize the numerous situations you encounter daily as occasions for improving competencies and actively improve your performance. In Case in Point 5.4 you participate in an exercise that enables you to connect course activities to specific skills.

STUDENT PORTFOLIOS

Perhaps your institution is one of an increasing number of colleges and universities that encourages or requires the creation of a portfolio. A portfolio is a technique (either electronic or hard copy) that enables you to reflect on your developmental progress throughout college, assemble evidence of your accomplishments, and identify the competences or skills your achievements represent. Portfolios may contain such documents as a short (five pages) autobiography, one-page mission or goals statement, job resume, major papers, artistic or technical products, evidence of computer or other technical skills, research projects, certificates of accomplishment, awards, job evaluations, and documents describing participation in clubs, volunteer work, athletics. View this portfolio as another type of transcript—a co-curricular transcript. Maintaining a portfolio provides personal satisfaction for having organized and documented your numerous activities. The portfolio is a tool for continued self-reflection in your progress toward personal and professional goals, and it serves as an interview tool for jobs or graduate and professional school.

To the extent you accurately connect specific competencies to your numerous activities, you will be ready for behaviorally-based interviews that seek specific evidence of particular skills (Evers and Schnarr 2002). For example, when an employer or graduate admission committee asks about your

CASE IN POINT 5.4   Competencies in the Classroom

If you are enrolled in a college or university where instruction is designed for the attainment of each level of several abilities or competencies (e.g., Alverno College of Milwaukee, Wisconsin, which pioneered a highly successful ability model), regard Case in Point 5.4 as optional reading. If your curriculum is not structured around a competency-based model, the following exercise using the four bases of competence will provide you with valuable insights.

Locate the syllabus and course materials for two courses you are currently taking, preferably in different disciplines or courses completed recently. Place the materials next to each other and compare with them with the 18 skills and our remarks below.

Communicating

Interpersonal
Every course consists of a group of individuals who should *interact* with each other (as well as with the instructor) in an open, respectful manner that promotes mutual learning in the achievement of common course goals. Recall Baxter Magolda's finding (chapter 4) that higher levels of post-college knowing were characterized by collaboration; the importance of the interpersonal dimension in Chickering and Reisser's vectors (chapter 3); and the roles of the interpersonal dimension in emotional and successful intelligence above. Except for those large, impersonal lecture classes where professors profess with minimal interaction, an essential ingredient of all courses is its social dimension. As you review the syllabi you have at hand, recall the extent to which the interpersonal dimension of communicating is (or was) important.

Listening
An essential skill in all courses, listening is the intentional attending to the instructor and classmates when they speak *and* the avoiding of distractions (talking, reading). To what extent are your listening skills influencing what you learn (or do not learn)?

Oral and Written Communication
Review your course materials and estimate the amount of emphasis (percent of the final grade) given to participation, oral reports, papers, and other written assignments. The value of "homework" to skill-building is not simply a function of how many or how much of the final grade they account for but also of the quality of instructor feedback and your decision to incorporate that feedback into your subsequent communications.

Managing Self

Learning
The first step to managing yourself is to acquire knowledge. You enrolled in the courses (even those required "GenEds") to gain knowledge you hope to use somehow and sometime in the near- or long-term future. How are you using the knowledge you acquired?

Personal Organization/ Time Management
You may have learned as a freshman, perhaps the hard way, that managing time and being organized are essential survival skills (they are in the workplace). As you review each set of materials, recall the importance of such skills for completing assignments on time at a quality level while managing other priorities. Did you improve these skills in subsequent academic terms?

CASE IN POINT 5.4   Continued

Personal Strengths
Also recall the importance that high energy, strong motivation, positive attitudes, stress management, and other personal strengths played in what you learned. Did different courses demand different strengths or different levels of these qualities? Were you required to dig very deeply into your psychological resources to accomplish your goals? Did your efforts strengthen these qualities?

Problem Solving/Analytic
This skill set is readily visible in a wide range of course activities when you analyze them into their component parts and the intellectual demands each assignment requires. When you were assigned a critical essay, math problems, a research project, a design problem, or when you chose a topic to present in class, your instructors may not have used the terms "problem solving," "analysis," "critical thinking," or "reasoning," but they expected you to engage in such activities. Did you use their feedback to improve these skills?

Managing People and Tasks

Coordinating
Busy students constantly coordinate course work, class schedules, jobs, family responsibilities, and social activities to accomplish what they need to. Group projects require thoughtful coordination and collaboration to effect a positive working environment. The professional world uses the term *multi-tasking* to describe the necessity for working on several projects simultaneously, often using different skills.

Decision Making
Everyday activities are filled with innumerable decisions that require a thoughtful assessment of their consequences. As a freshman you may have chosen a course, job, friend, or social activity with insufficient data (e.g., a classmate's opinion) to support your decision and paid even less attention to the consequences of your decision. As an advanced student, you now study the course syllabus carefully on the first day, anticipate the work load, and use tacit knowledge and past experiences, (in addition to classmates' opinions) to project the kind of relationship you will have with the instructor. You try to determine how the course fits with your interests and career plans. As you review your course materials, try to ascertain the ways that your decision making has improved during the past two years.

Leadership/Influence
Leadership is an achievable skill for the ordinary person; most people can learn to guide, direct, and lead by example, if they work at it. Recall the importance of leadership in the Evers et al. survey of graduates and their supervisors. To what extent do you try to influence others in your courses, whether sharing your experiences and views in a discussion or accepting responsibilities in a group project?

Managing Conflict
Your recollection of emotional intelligence reminds you that awareness, understanding, integrating, and regulating emotions (the components of EI) are certainly ingredients of conflict management. Recall the types of conflict you experienced in the courses used for this exercise (e.g., disputes with the instructor or fellow students, overwhelming or ambiguous assignments, conflicts with other priorities) and the ways you identified

(Continued)

CASE IN POINT 5.4   Continued

and dealt with them. Were the conflicts resolved satisfactorily? The patterns of conflict resolution you use will probably continue to be used in your subsequent personal and professional life; work at making these patterns effective.

Planning and Organizing
These two skills focus specifically on work tasks and personal organization. Review course syllabi and materials. To the extent that you can effectively analyze course assignments into their intellectual and physical requirements, anticipate time and resources needed, monitor progress, and revise your plans as needed, you are practicing skills essential for success in intense, multi-tasked environments.

Mobilizing Innovation and Change

Evers and his associates believe the final two bases of competence are the ones most sought by employers and least developed by graduates. When you apply the four skills contained in this category to your coursework, the classroom may pale in contrast to the boardroom, but many college courses afford opportunities to establish the following competencies.

Ability to Conceptualize
An honors course, research or independent study, or capstone project/paper requires original work in one form or another. Typically you identify and sift through numerous resources (e.g., conducting a literature search), integrate the information into a hypothesis or problem, collect data or create a product, and draw conclusions that have implications for future work. Along the way you will probably run into roadblocks, discover new aspects of the problem to investigate, and change your original plans. This process of discovery requires conceptualizing and reformulating

ideas, procedures, and outcomes; it represents a highly transferable skill prized by many employers. The challenge is to transfer your skills and experiences to new problem situations.

Creativity/Innovation/Change
Although these three terms are not synonymous, this skill set combines with conceptualization and risk-taking to stimulate thinking and problem solving in nontraditional ways that force a person to "think outside the box." To what extent do your courses intentionally promote creative thinking through readings, discussions, assignments, field trips, or experiential activities? Are you encouraged to find new ways to interpret a literary character, test a hypothesis, render ideas artistically, solve a technical problem, or apply abstract concepts to a social problem?

Risk-Taking
Each course involves several types of risks, including the subject matter, workloads, relevance to personal and professional growth, and your relations with the instructor and classmates. To what extent do you evaluate these risks as reasonable, goal-related, and beneficial to future decisions?

Visioning
What will your groups or organizations be doing in one or two years? In what ways can you influence the direction of your family? The social organizations of which you are a member? Your circle of friends? The organization in which you are employed?

In many respects your college experiences are vastly different from those you will encounter in the future. When you analyze how the 18 competencies are reflected in coursework however, it becomes apparent that many academic activities teach skills analogous to those identified by Evers and his

---

CASE IN POINT 5.4   Continued

associates and in *Recruiting Trends 2002–2003*. Your college education can provide you (if you actively take advantage of it) with an infrastructure of skill sets needed for your future professional and personal success. Your job is to (1) understand the competences and how they are represented in coursework, and (2) make it your goal to practice (with feedback) the complex behaviors the skills represent. That's hard work, but

its potential payoff is well worth the effort. The *Competencies in the Classroom* required considerable time and thought from you. We hope it generated insights you can ponder and use during your passage from college to post-college cultures. By the way, do not be surprised to find a good connection between the mastery of these competencies and the kind of grades that are rewarded with scholarships.

---

ability to coordinate activities and work with others, you can present evaluations from your employer, documents that testify to your involvement in campus activities, or a copy of the Power Point presentation you created with classmates for a group project.

Have you noticed that the perspectives on intelligence share some common threads? Journal Starter 2 encourages you to compare successful intelligence with EI and the bases of competence and explore the ideas they share. We hope these perspectives expand your thinking about what it really means to be smart, and we conclude with a brief look at still another context in which intelligent behavior is crucial. The following perspective is an example of how an *absence* of tacit knowledge and practical intelligence can lead to poor decisions.

A PRIMER ON
PERSONAL INDEPENDENCE

By the time students reach their junior or senior year, many live somewhat independently of their family and university. They may drive a car (with maintenance and insurance costs), share a house or apartment (with a lease and cost-sharing responsibilities), hold a job (with its rewards and demands), or attend school in another country. For other students, moving out of home or residence hall, buying a car, working full-time, and moving to a large city or small town will be a shock. Like white-water rafting, rock climbing, or high-altitude hiking, living independently is an exciting but risky adventure. You cannot afford to make costly mistakes during your transition from college because positive experiences in your personal life help promote success on the job. Are you confident in your knowledge and skills to handle these issues?

- Leases: Are you willing to sign a lease for a house or apartment without the assistance of an attorney? Will you have the good sense to purchase renter's insurance? And if your rowdy roommate throws a party that destroys the place on a weekend that you are gone, who is responsible for repairs?

■ Job Benefits: When you visit the human resources office on the first day of work, will you feel confident about allocating your benefits? For example, how much life insurance do you really need if no one depends on you? Do you know the difference between a 401k, a 403b, and an IRA? Are there strings attached to the company tuition-reimbursement plan?

■ Health Insurance: What type of coverage is offered by your employer, and is it enough? Do you know the difference between a PPO, HMO, and PCP? A college grad and Texas native learned the hard way that uninsured people may pay more for medical costs than organizations pay. Her two-day stay in a Brooklyn, NY hospital for an appendectomy left her with $19,000 in medical bills (Lagnado 2003). Ugh!

■ Credit Cards: If you do not use credit cards, you cannot build a revolving-credit history. Without a credit history, you may have trouble renting an apartment or getting a car loan; you may pay premium prices for insurance and cell phones; and you will not have a standard against which a potential employer can judge your character and reliability (Yarrow 2002). On the other hand, if you abuse your credit cards, you create a negative credit history and encounter similar problems. Now is the time to teach yourself about using credit cards wisely.

■ Automobiles: You may not want to buy your parents' model, but can you truly depend on your friends' evaluations of cars? A car is usually the second most expensive consumer purchase (next to a house), so you will want to research it carefully using magazines such as *Consumer Reports* or websites such as *edmunds.com*.

■ Product Purchases: Living independently means buying new products. When you spend hundreds of dollars of your hard-earned money for a DVD player, bicycle, microwave oven, computer, digital camera, TV, and similar items, how do you know if you are receiving quality products with the features you want at a good price? And there *are* differences among cell-phone plans, pregnancy test kits, water filters, restaurants, treadmills, and hospital services. Each of these products or services, along with several others, was evaluated in *Consumer Reports* monthly magazine in a recent year. The annual April auto issue is one of the most respected sources for purchasing an automobile. The cost of a year's subscription can be recovered easily in one wise purchase.

A search of your local bookstores and the web should lead to good (and not so good) resources that teach you intelligent behavior in daily living. At the end of this chapter are a few representative websites on issues listed previously. Following are a few paperback books, listed in alphabetical order, and recommended for your perusal.

Ellen Braitman: *Dollars & Sense for College Students or How Not to Run Out of Money by Midterms.* New York: Princeton Review Publishing Co. 1998. www.randomhouse.com

Cap & Compass: *life after school. explained.* www.CapandCompass.com.

Sarah Young and Susan Shelly: *The Complete Idiot's Guide to Personal Finance in Your 20s and 30s* (2ed.). Indianapolis, IN: Alpha Books. 2002. www.idiotsguides.com

CONCLUDING COMMENTS

Being smart means, in part, recognizing that intelligence does not reveal itself in any one manner. Test scores, course grades, and GPAs are primarily manifestations of the essential analytic-thinking tools and experiences that colleges and universities nurture so well in their students. Sternberg expands the elusive concept of intelligence by including creative and practical aspects that operate in balance with analytical intelligence as you struggle to shape the environment around your strengths and limitations. Although you probably received no formal instruction in emotional intelligence, you could view college as a continuous, self-taught, non-credit course in recognizing, understanding, and managing emotions. Similarly, while you listened to lectures, mastered math, absorbed art, and focused on French, you were quietly developing an array of marketable competences that should transfer to life and career. Finally, when you begin your full-time encounter with the "real world," be knowledgeable about those apparently mundane but important dimensions of daily living.

JOURNAL STARTERS

1. On the horizontal position of a sheet of paper, create four columns: *successful intelligence, emotional intelligence, bases of competence,* and *seven vectors* (from chapter 3). Review the main points contained in these four perspectives, then note under each column the terms or concepts that are common to any two or more perspectives.

2. Think about a person whom you respect deeply for his/her emotional intelligence or maturity. Describe the behaviors and qualities that characterize that person, and then compare the terms you used with the list of 10 EI behaviors. Optional: Do the same for an individual whom you judge deficient in EI.

3. Several examples were given that showed how concepts of successful intelligence, emotional intelligence, and the bases of competence could be applied to everyday activities. There are few courses, workshops, or structured learning opportunities designed to raise awareness of and practice these abilities and skills. Try to identify specific instances or opportunities in your residence, social, and work settings, however, where students could recognize and strengthen these forms of intelligent behavior. (The exercise in Case in Point 5.4 applies the bases of competence to coursework).

4. What are the most significant insights you gained from reading this chapter that you can you apply to your life? What questions remain unanswered?

FYI

www.ConsumerReports.org—intended mainly for subscribers, but it lists the types of products and consumer issues presented in its monthly magazine

www.creditalk.com—lots of information about credit issues

www.nolo.com—bills itself as "everyday law for everyday people" with software, books, and forms, including a tenant's legal guide

www.springstreet.com—provides access to thousands of rentals plus practical tips about moving, pets, insurance, and more

REFERENCES

Bridges, W. (1994). *Job shift: How to prosper in a workplace without jobs.* Reading, MA: Addison-Wesley.

Career Services and Placement/Collegiate Employment Research Institute. (2002). *2002–2003 recruiting trends.* East Lansing, MI: Michigan State University.

Ciarrochi, J., Forgas, J. P., and Mayer, J. D. (2001). *Emotional intelligence in everyday life: A scientific inquiry.* Philadelphia, PA: Psychology Press.

Evers, F. T., Rush J. C., and Berdrow, I. (1998). *The bases of competence: Skills for lifelong learning and employability.* San Francisco: Jossey-Bass.

Evers, F., and Schnarr. L., (2002). The Bases of Competence skills model: A Framework for leadership education. Paper presented at the annual conference of the International Leadership Association. Seattle, WA.

Goleman, D. (1998). *Working with emotional intelligence.* NY: Bantam Books.

Hettich, P. (1998). *Learning skills for college and career* (2ed). Pacific Grove, CA: Brooks/Cole.

Lagnado, L. (2003, March 17). Full price: A young woman, an appendectomy, and a $19,000 debt. *The Wall Street Journal* pp. A1, A7.

Mayer, J. D., Caruso, D., and Salovey, P. (1999). Emotional intelligence meets traditional standards for an intelligence. *Intelligence,* 27: 267–298.

Stern, L. (2003). Stop! Do Not Turn the Page!, *How to Get Into College: 2004 Edition.* pp. 44–47. New York: *Newsweek,* Inc., Kaplan, Inc.

Sternberg, R. J. (1996). *Successful intelligence: How practical and creative intelligence determine success in life.* NY: Simon & Schuster.

Sternberg, R. J. (1999). The theory of Successful Intelligence. *Review of General Psychology* 3(4): 292–316.

Yarrow, L. (2002, April 26). Soaring into financial independence. *Chicago Tribune,* Section 13, pp. 1, 4.

6

⌒

Motivation
and Learning

Principles That Work
When You Do

Motivation is when your dreams put on work clothes.

PARKES ROBINSON

Rather than learn in preparation for work, employees must learn their way
out of the work problems they address.

NANCY M. DIXON

If you are the typical college junior or senior, you have spent a minimum of
15 years in the educational workplace to prepare for life and the career of
your dreams. During that time you acquired specific *strategies* for learning
course material, passing tests, solving problems, and interacting with others.
Sometimes these strategies worked; sometimes they did not. Your success or
failure with these strategies is influenced by several factors, including the
motivational energy you direct to each activity. You may think the learning and
motivational processes that work for you during college will work for you in
the workplace and that your task during your remaining time in college is to
fine-tune these skills for a good job. Recall, however, that the participants in
Baxter Magolda's study (1992) did not develop independent and contextual
knowing until after college. Also recall Philip Gardner's observation (1998)
that most graduates are deficient in skills and experiences required to navigate
the social dimensions of work. Finally, remember Ed Holton's assertion (1998)
that the learning processes for which students are rewarded in college are different from those needed for success on the job. For example, college students

expect regular feedback, correct answers, and freedom to choose their level of performance; in the workplace feedback is infrequent, uncertainty is the norm, and "A" level performance is always expected.

If new college graduates are not prepared, as these researchers claim, should you really expect your "tried and true" strategies to automatically transfer successfully to your next full-time job? Probably not! You need not become overly anxious by this possibility, however, IF you do two things. First, take advantage of the numerous opportunities on and off campus to acquire the experiences and skills needed in your future work. Second, pursue your daily activities with the conviction you are in the business of lifelong learning. Your education is *your job.* You are a self-employed businessperson, like an entrepreneur without a secretary, whose job is to achieve a college education. Not only are the wages for this job deferred for many years, you pay good money to be part of your organization. These suggestions, along with the other ideas presented in this chapter, can mentally prepare you to put on the work clothes of your dreams. You will be introduced to key concepts of motivation and learning derived from research and practice in the field of organizational behavior. If you understand how motivational and learning processes operate in work environments, we believe you can apply this knowledge to your college and post-college workplaces. Finally, you will benefit by acting on the wisdom of Ralph Waldo Emerson, "Nothing great was ever achieved without enthusiasm."

MOTIVATION: DONNING DREAMS
IN WORK CLOTHES

Motivation refers to those processes that arouse and direct your mental activity and behavior toward a particular goal. It is the degree of passion you experience for pursuing an activity. Motives explain the causes of your behavior—why you do what you do. Some motives are simple, but most often and especially in social contexts, motives are multifaceted. If motives represent the dressing of your dreams in work clothes, as Parkes Robinson claims, then you should become familiar with a wardrobe of motivational concepts you can wear to your college job.

INTRINSIC AND EXTRINSIC MOTIVES:
WHO'S THE BOSS?

Extrinsic motives are those where the arousal and directing of motivational energy originate in sources *outside* the individual. In contrast, the arousal and direction of intrinsic motives originate from *within* the person, from within you. For example, when you were a first-year student, what goals motivated you to be in college? Be honest.

	Yes	No
■ To have a good time with new friends?	_____	_____
■ To prepare for a career?	_____	_____
■ To satisfy the wishes of family and friends?	_____	_____
■ To develop intellectual and social skills?	_____	_____
■ To avoid having to work a full-time job?	_____	_____
■ To learn more about the world?	_____	_____

If you checked "Yes" to the first, third, and fifth items, you may have been extrinsically motivated; the source of your motivational arousal came from sources outside of you, such as family and friends. If you checked "Yes" to the second, fourth, and sixth items, the source of arousal probably originated from within you. Intrinsically motivated people (intrinsics) enjoy the *process* of learning for the sake of learning, be it career preparation, skill development, or learning about the world. The extrinsically motivated person, or extrinsic, is aroused by others to act or acts in order to avoid something perceived as unpleasant, such as the full-time job or the loss of peer and family support. If you waited several years to start college, chances are you were intrinsically motivated because intrinsic motivation usually emerges with experience, maturity, and age.

For many students progress toward academic success and emotional maturity during college is often a matter of shifting from primarily extrinsic to primarily intrinsic motives. The extrinsic studies primarily to get a grade, whereas the intrinsic studies to learn, as well as to receive a grade. The intrinsic is likely to persist and overcome such barriers as "killer" classes, growing debt, personal crisis, failure, complicated relationships, and a dead-end job. Why? The energy that arouses and directs his or her actions is generated from inside, like a psychological power plant; it is not "second-hand," coming from other people. Not only does intrinsic motivation sustain you through the gauntlet of personal challenges in the college workplace it prepares you to manage the larger obstacles you will encounter during graduate or professional school or in your first jobs. In the workplace intrinsic motivation enables you to deal as long as you can with the low starting salary, long hours, continual changes, lack of promotion, poor supervision, irritating co-workers, or poor working conditions—when you have to. Intrinsic motives energize you to seek excellence and recognition for as long as you want. Studies have shown that the stress and medical risks associated with work have less to do with the quantity of work and more to do with one's attitude toward it. So if you are not yet intrinsically motivated, make it your goal to become the origin of your own motives and actions, not to be the pawn of others. Be patient with the process and recognize that the shift to intrinsic motives certainly does not eliminate all extrinsic motives. No one is a "super-intrinsic" because there is no perfect work environment. For instance, you may be a highly competent, self-confident, intrinsically motivated employee. However, if your supervisor is apathetic about important issues in your department and does not care whether you loaf or labor, it is very difficult to remain intrinsically motivated.

If you are motivated about most of the things you do, most of the time, congratulate yourself for this fortunate condition. If you lack motivation about college, your academic major, or life in general, several factors can contribute to your feelings, including lack of goals, poor grades, stress, normal psychosocial development (recall comments in chapter 3 about the stages of identity), poor relationships, or depression. Give serious consideration to consulting with a counselor. If you are not involved in co-curricular activities, join an organization. Volunteer activities, athletics, campus organizations, and academic clubs can be wonderful opportunities for learning a little more about yourself and uncovering hidden interests that sometimes take on a life of their own. The following pages describe three popular theories of workplace motivation derived from research and practice that you can apply to the college workplace.

IF YOU DON'T KNOW WHERE YOU ARE GOING, HOW DO YOU KNOW WHEN YOU ARRIVE?— MOTIVATION THROUGH GOAL SETTING

As we defined motivation as the arousal and direction of mental processes toward a goal, let's begin at the end—with goals. You have goals; otherwise you would not be reading this book. One of your life's goals is to *achieve* (not receive) a college education that prepares you personally and professionally for life. Some goals, such as recognition by your profession or enjoying a middle- or upper-class life-style are long-range goals that usually require several years to attain. Intermediate goals, such as achieving your college education, gaining entry into graduate school, or owning a new car, may require only a few years to accomplish. Day-to-day living requires that you establish short-term goals that can be accomplished within a year, such as improving grades, finding a better job, getting along with a roommate, or taking a vacation.

The Goal-Setting theory developed by Edwin Locke and Gary Latham states that employees are motivated to work when they can compare their current performance with a standard (a goal) they seek to achieve for success. Performance below the standard presumably leads to greater effort to correct the deficiency; performance at or above the standard produces feelings of accomplishment. Setting goals can enhance motivation when three conditions are met:

- Goals must be *specific.*
- Goals must be *realistic* or achievable.
- You must receive *feedback* about your performance (Greenberg and Baron 2000).

First, goals must be stated in specific terms and measurable if possible. For example, the procrastinating first-semester senior who needs an internship to graduate may say, "I'll look into it next week," but probably won't, regardless of good intentions. Instead the student should have established a specific goal (a semester earlier), such as "Next Monday I will begin the process of seeking an internship in an organization like the State Department in preparation for my career goal of working in a foreign country." This goal is specific about when the process begins (next week), the type of organization (for example, the State Department), and the purpose of the internship (to prepare for a career in a foreign country). Typically, goals consist of sub-goals that must be accomplished in order to reach the final goal. Identifying sub-goals enables you to simultaneously create a timely plan of action and determine the reality of achieving the final goal. In this example the appropriate sub-goals could have included the following: begin to plan at least one full semester in advance, download internship information from websites, review university policies, and meet with the academic and foreign-study advisors. These sub-goals are sufficiently specific to permit a comparison between the student's planned and actual activities.

Secondly, goals must be realistic and attainable. If your specific goal is too easy to reach, it becomes meaningless; if it is too difficult, you become discouraged. Performing a reality check may require honest feedback from an advisor, friend, or family member. For instance, if your GPA is well below the minimum required or if you are afraid to leave home, is it realistic to apply for study abroad? If you are a parent of small children, what are the consequences of being gone from your family for four months? Or taking them with you? Each of these situations could become a positive challenge to overcome, but a reality check is prerequisite to successful goal setting.

The third step in the process is to obtain regular feedback about the specific activities you attempted. If you create a "do-list" of your sub-goals, you can cross each one off the list when it is completed and experience the pleasant feeling that follows small accomplishments.

Goal Setting and Self-Regulation

When you set goals, you are attempting to regulate your own behavior—to take charge. Self-regulation, according to psychologist Albert Bandura, consists of four interrelated *processes,* some of which are reflected in the previous three steps. These processes focus on beliefs and feelings, and they influence how well you use goals to modify your motivation (Donovan 2001).

Goal Establishment Goal establishment is the process of setting standards for yourself that represent a desired set of circumstances or behaviors. These standards must be specific, realistic, and amenable to providing feedback. The standards you set will be based jointly on your past experience and your self-efficacy (i.e., your belief that you can succeed at a particular task). For instance, if you have traveled widely, successfully, and derived considerable satisfaction from your travel experiences, the goal to study abroad is probably realistic. Self-efficacy is very important because if you believe you can succeed at a task such as foreign travel, chances are you will be motivated to try it. Without positive self-efficacy, chances are you'll spend another academic term on your campus.

Self-Observation Once you set a goal, you should *actively* monitor your progress in reaching it. If you plan to study abroad during the first term of your senior year, what steps are you taking to prepare the way, and are you taking them in a timely manner? If you plan to take a year off before entering graduate or professional school, what information have you obtained about the graduate programs and application deadlines, what kind of job will you seek for the interim, and what kinds of activities along the way will enhance your application? In short, pay close attention to the progress you are making (or not making) in reaching your sub-goals and goals.

Self-Evaluation Self-observation is followed by self-evaluation, the process that allows you to compare your actual progress with your intended progress. Are you ahead of, behind, or on schedule? Honest and objective self-evaluation enables you to adjust your activities appropriately to reach the standard you set. Self-observation and self-evaluation require individuals to reflect and confront themselves. Mark Twain observed, "Reflection is the beginning of reform. There can be no reform without reflection."

Self-Reaction The information you gather about the goals you set, your self-observation, and your self-evaluation produce positive or negative reactions. Being ahead of schedule or on time represents a positive discrepancy from your goal that creates good feelings and higher self-efficacy; falling behind schedule represents a negative discrepancy that produces bad feelings and lower self-efficacy with regard to that aspect of the goal. Your feelings about your progress in attaining goals are very important, and they affect your motivation. If you are reaching your goal ahead of schedule or on time, you may be motivated to set slightly higher standards and push yourself further. If you are falling behind, you may work harder to close the gap, reassess or change your strategy, lower your standards, or even give up.

In summary, setting specific and realistic goals can arouse and direct your energies to compare what you want to do (your goals) and what you actually do. When your performance matches your goals, pat yourself on the back and watch your self-efficacy rise; when it does not, review the goal-setting steps and processes in the context of your situation, and make appropriate adjustments.

We encourage you to establish specific and realistic long-range, intermediate-range, and short-range goals in the personal and social dimensions of your life. Also, set goals for the pleasant activities that you want to do, not simply for the tasks that you must do. Setting goals is an excellent way to strengthen intrinsic motivation because *you* determine which goals are realistic for you, *you* monitor their progress; *you* become accountable for your actions, and *you* plan subsequent goals. Furthermore, establishing goals prepares you for the diverse workplaces you are likely to encounter. Many corporations and not-for-profit organizations use goal-setting to assign tasks to employees, to monitor and evaluate performance, and to determine salary increases. In some organizations, supervisors assign goals to employees; in others, employees work collaboratively with supervisors to establish goals. In short, goal setting is a very valuable tool in your business of lifelong learning.

Take a few minutes and practice this technique. Think of one, short-range, personal, social, or academic goal that you want to attain during the next four, six, or twelve months.

1. My specific goal is to _____

   What specific tasks must I perform to reach that goal?

   _____

2. Why is this goal realistic? _____

   If the goal is not realistic, what can I do to make it realistic?_____

   _____

3. What steps will I take to monitor this goal? _____

   _____

Why not make it your goal to use this tool for such activities as reducing stress, planning a career, getting to know someone better, exercising, joining a club or social activity, investigating graduate or professional school, improving contact with family or friends, or planning a trip.

A word of caution! Most goals that students set operate on a week-to-week, month-to-month, or semester-to-semester timeframe. If you wait until your last academic term to plan life after college, you may miss several excellent opportunities.

FAIR ENOUGH!
THE EQUITY PERSPECTIVE

According to J. Stacy Adams' Equity Theory, our motivation is influenced by comparisons we make between our performance and that of others. We mentally calculate a ratio of our work outcomes (such as grades, salary, or recognition) to our inputs (such as time spent, effort, or skills) (Greenberg and Baron, 2000). Because the theory can be complicated, consider this example that many students have experienced. You devoted the previous weekend to studying for your first calculus test. You are overjoyed to learn when your exam is returned that your score of 98 percent earned you an "A." You conclude that the input of your time and effort was equitably rewarded by your sense of accomplishment and the "A" you received (the outcomes), *until* a glance across the desks on either side of you reveals that scores of 85 percent and 88 percent also earned an "A." You feel cheated! Your outcome ("A") when compared to your input is unequal to that of your classmates who received the same grade for, apparently, less effort and/or knowledge. You experience *underpayment inequity* in relation to your classmates and feel angry. Your peers may experience *overpayment inequity* and a tinge of guilt when they discover their substantially lower scores also received an "A". Don't expect their guilt to last nearly as long as your anger!

Motivation often diminishes when people *perceive* that inequities exist. If you perceived the previous situation as unfair, what might your attitude be toward studying for the next exam? Toward the material you once enjoyed learning? Toward the instructor? Toward your peers? Do not allow negative feelings created by your perception of inequity to change your attitudes or behavior. You will derive no benefits from cutting classes, blaming your classmates, castigating the teacher, or cheating on the next exam. You must summon your intrinsic motivation to help you "bite the bullet" and adapt, clarify your goals, continue your hard work, and ask the teacher about this apparent inequity. We used the terms "apparent inequity" because it is possible that your instructor has a rational explanation for giving an "A" to such discrepant scores.

Equity theory enables us to understand the impact of misunderstandings on motivation and performance. It is important for teachers and supervisors to articulate standards of performance and promote equity in the classroom and in the workplace. It is equally important for students and employees to withhold judgment about perceived inequities until they have the facts. Equity is essential in the relationships between coach and player, student and resident hall assistant, supervisor and employee, spouses, and any situation where people pass judgment on others' work, grades, skill level, position, or personal behavior. When people believe that they are being treated fairly, they are willing to work hard. By now you are mature enough to know that life is filled with inequities that sometimes cannot be avoided or resolved. If your energy and commitment are diminished by a perception of unfairness, however, seek the perspectives of others you respect, gather the facts, and meet with the teacher or supervisor to discuss the issue objectively.

In the corporate workplace, you are likely to encounter and perceive (correctly or incorrectly) inequities in such matters as salary, job assignment, promotion, recognition, support, salary increases, office space, accessibility to superiors, training opportunities, and status. These inequities may be based on seniority, age, race, gender, social skills, relationships, or the processes used to reach decisions. Recognize that your perceptions could be influenced by the facts of the situation *or* by your limited experience or unrealistic expectations, including feelings of entitlement. According to Kim and Mauborgne (2003), employees "care as much about the fairness of the process through which an outcome is produced as they do about the outcome itself" (p. 130). They are willing to cooperate and trust the system, even when they disagree with it, if the process is fair. While in college, become aware of how inequities affect your motivation and performance and develop healthy strategies for dealing with them.

In the space below, recall a situation where you believe that you were treated unfairly.

Situation:_____

_____

In what ways, if any, did this actual or perceived inequity (the distinction is very important) change

    your attitudes or behavior?_____

    your level of motivation?_____

What did you do to recover from the situation?_____

Repeat these questions for a situation where you thought you had been treated unfairly, but subsequently discovered that you were wrong.

Situation:_____
In what ways, if any, did this actual or perceived inequity change

    your attitudes or behavior?_____

    your level of motivation?_____

What did you do to recover from this situation?_____

GREAT EXPECTATIONS

Often, motivation rises or falls because of expectations we have about a particular event or activity. The student who discovered that scores of 85 percent, 88 percent, and 98 percent each received an "A" implicitly *expected* that lower scores would result in lower grades. Chances are the students who received an 85 percent and 88 percent probably expected a "B," not an "A." The expectancy theory of motivation developed by Victor Vroom and others states that an employees' motivation is comprised of three beliefs or expectations about their work.

- A person's effort will influence his/her performance (*expectancy belief*).
- The performance will be rewarded appropriately (*instrumentality belief,* i.e., performance is instrumental to receiving a reward).
- The rewards have a particular value or *valence* to the individual (Greenberg and Baron 2000).

Expectancy, instrumentality, and valence combine in a multiplicative way (the value of each factor is multiplied by other factors) to generate your level of motivation. Chances are you have used the expectancy theory of motivation many times to decide how to allocate your time and efforts to a particular task. Consider the following example. Mike has a limited amount of time during a two-day period to write a report for environmental biology and to prepare a 15-minute speech for his political science course. Mike knows that science is his hard subject, that he will have to write at least two drafts of the paper before it is acceptable, that the teacher is a hard grader, and that this course is only a general education requirement. His expectancy belief may be at a moderate level because he thinks that his efforts will, after a couple of time-consuming drafts, ultimately lead to a satisfactory report. His instrumentality belief will be at a low level because he believes that, even if he works hard, he probably will not get a high grade. Finally, because he believes that the knowledge and grade he obtains in this required course are not very important, his valence belief is also at a low level. Using a five-point scale where 1 = very low, 3 = moderate, and 5 = very high, we can (for instructional purposes) represent Mike's motivation to write the environmental biology paper this way.

Expectancy $\times$ Instrumentality $\times$ Valence = Motivation
      3        $\times$ 2 $\times$ 2   = 12 (of possible 125)

Mike's motivation for preparing the political science speech is a very different story. He is skilled at public speaking; he is doing well in a course in which the teacher is known to be somewhat lenient; and the course relates closely to his pre-law program. Mike firmly believes the time he spends to prepare the speech will strongly affect his performance (expectancy is very high); he believes that a good speech will be amply rewarded by the teacher (instrumentality is very high), and he believes that a high grade in this course will look good on his transcript (valence is high). We could represent Mike's motivation for preparing the speech this way.

Expectancy $\times$ Instrumentality $\times$ Valence = Motivation
      5        $\times$ 5 $\times$ 4   = 100 (of a possible 125)

Mike will actually enjoy preparing the speech, but he will dig deep to arouse and direct energy (our definition of motivation) to writing the science report—it will be pure drudgery! The political science speech and environmental biology report are almost at opposite ends of Mike's motivational spectrum. Consider what happens to the numerical representations of his motivation if Mike's three beliefs were different. For instance, how would you describe Mike's level of motivation if he did not like public speaking and the expectancy value was at 2 instead of 5? Or if Mike assigned a valence of 5 to the environmental biology course (thinking the course might be valuable later in his law practice)? If Mike chose not to write the science report, i.e., expectancy = 0, his motivation score would be 0, since the three beliefs are multiplicatively connected, and he would receive an "F" for that assignment. Again, remember that the application of numbers to represent motivational levels is not a true quantitative relationship, but a device for illustrating this concept.

The expectancy theory illustrates the power that beliefs, attitudes, and past experiences can have on our energy and efforts. It shows us how past failures or successes with particular tasks, external factors (e.g., the hard-nosed vs. the lenient teacher), and rewards shape and direct motivation. Much of the time we are not conscious of these elements. If you can analyze your reasons for performing an assignment using the three belief components, perhaps you can monitor why you do what you do and change the situation, when it becomes necessary. Finally, you may better understand the role that intrinsic and extrinsic rewards occupy in your beliefs and behaviors.

It is important to acknowledge that a person's performance on a specific task or in college is not simply the combination of the three motivational beliefs. Abilities, skills, traits, and opportunities are other powerful determinants of success. You may be strongly motivated to become another Colin Powell, acquire the wealth of Bill Gates, or play tennis like the Williams sisters, but without the successful combination of abilities, skills, personal characteristics, and opportunities these individuals possess, your best efforts and intense desires will be insufficient. You may be highly motivated to become a quantum physicist, but if your math and science skills are poor due to inadequate academic preparation or lack of innate ability, motivation alone will not lead you to your goal. Use the remaining academic terms to correct your deficiencies or, if that is not possible, thoughtfully search other career paths.

Place yourself in each of the situations below and explain how the three beliefs would influence your motivation.

Expectancy Compare the expectancy beliefs of the employee who daily uses state-of-the-art technology to that of the person who must use grossly outdated equipment.

Compare the expectancy beliefs of two air conditioner sales representatives, one whose territory is Dallas/Fort Worth while the other's is western Montana.

Compare the expectancy beliefs of the new employee whose supervisor is perceived as a Charles Dickens' Ebenezer Scrooge (before his three "spirit therapy" sessions on Christmas eve) with that of the new employee whose supervisor is highly admired and respected.

Instrumentality Imagine working in one organization where the most and least productive employees earn about the same salary versus an organization that gives bonuses for high productivity or uses a pay-for-performance system.

Valence In today's diverse organizations, not everyone wants the same benefits. You may not be interested in the childcare benefit that your co-worker raves about, but you strongly appreciate the company's tuition reimbursement program so you can take graduate courses. Many companies offer a cafeteria-style benefits plan that lets employees choose their fringe benefits.

To gain additional practice with the three motivational beliefs, identify a project or assignment (academic, job-related, co-curricular) that you must complete within the next few weeks. Analyze how your beliefs might combine to influence your motivation to complete it. You could choose an assignment that you are looking forward to complete or one that you would like to avoid. Or you could complete this exercise twice for both assignments and then compare them.

Describe each belief and then assign it a numerical value that best represents it. Use a scale where "1" represents a Very Low level, "3" a Moderate level, and "5" "Very High"

Assignment:_____

Expectancy: The extent to which you believe that your effort influences your performance. _____ Value = _____

Instrumentality: The extent to which you believe that your performance will be rewarded: _____ Value = _____

Valence: The extent to which you value the rewards that you will receive _____ Value = _____

Multiply the 3 values to obtain a score: _____

Are there steps you can take to raise the value of your expectancy belief? For example, do you need additional resources (human, technical), knowledge, or assignment-related skills? Are there steps you can take to raise the value of the instrumentality belief? For instance, are there knowledge and skills you can transfer from this assignment to other settings? If the person controlling the rewards is stingy with them, can you become intrinsically motivated to complete the task with a positive attitude?

In summary, if you want to excel at whatever you do, learn to understand the factors that energize and direct your behavior. Four perspectives (Intrinsic Motivation, Goal Setting, Equity Theory, Expectancy Theory) explain how motivation operates in the workplace. Try on these work clothes in your college workplace. We cannot guarantee their fit, only that they are worth trying on. If these perspectives are useful now, chances are they will fit even better after college—whether your next workplace is just a job, a step to a career, or the career of your dreams.

PRACTICAL PRINCIPLES
OF WORKPLACE LEARNING

While motives arouse and direct our behavior, *learning* refers to those relatively permanent changes in thinking or behavior that result from our experiences. We spend a lifetime learning how to integrate information and apply it to our daily tasks. Throughout college your instructors have taught you various approaches to critical thinking, including reasoning, analysis, and problem solving. Mastery of critical thinking skills is absolutely essential to professional and personal success. In the remaining pages, however, you will focus on learning concepts that affect work-related attitudes, beliefs, and behaviors in ordinary activities that occur during college and in your transition. Two of the three topics of learning to be addressed are familiar to anyone who completed a general psychology course. Operant (instrumental) learning and observational learning (modeling) describe how habits and behaviors are established and maintained. The third topic is a model of experiential learning that may help you understand how you approach everyday problem situations.

Learning from Consequences

In *operant learning,* the real or anticipated consequences of your behavior can change the probability of that behavior's occurrence. Essentially, what you learn is strongly influenced by its consequences. One consequence of a particular behavior is *positive reinforcement* that increases the probability that the same or similar behavior will reoccur when conditions are appropriate. *Aversive* consequences reduce the attractiveness of a particular behavior (Halonen and Santrock 1996). Much of what we learn is accomplished without reinforcers; sometimes receiving external rewards discourages the learning process. However, so many of our habits and daily activities are maintained by operant learning that it is easy to ignore or devalue the ways that rewards and punishments shape our thoughts and actions. Consider a few examples that apply to college and career workplaces alike.

- The aversive consequences of arriving late to work or class (a reprimand, angry looks) decrease the probability that you will arrive late in the future.
- The positive consequences of remaining after class or work to help someone in need increase the probability that you may do the same when the situation arises again.
- The aversive consequences of falling behind in a class or job assignment (criticism, low grade, poor performance evaluation) increase the probability that you will work more efficiently on subsequent assignments (or they decrease the probability that you will fall behind again).
- The positive consequences of ending your smoking habit (better health, increased sense of self-control, friendlier friends) increase the probability that you will resist temptation to light up the next time you want to.
- The negative consequences of driving well beyond the speed limit (traffic ticket, risk of accident) increase the probability that you will drive safely.

Just as there are intrinsic and extrinsic motives, so too some rewards originate within ourselves (intrinsic), while others are delivered from external sources as the previous examples illustrate.

Take a few minutes to identify some of your ordinary behaviors or beliefs that are strongly influenced by their consequences. List the specific behavior or belief, the specific consequences (rewarding or aversive), and whether the probability of repeating the behavior is increased or decreased by your actions.

Behavior or Belief   Consequences   Probable Type of Change

_____

_____

_____

We are oversimplifying the process of operant learning to a degree for purposes of illustrating this concept. To demonstrate the pervasiveness of rewards in work settings, however, consider some examples used by employers that Bob Nelson identifies in his book *1001 Ways to Reward Employees* (1994).

- letters, cards, personal visits, or phone calls thanking employees
- recognition lunches, team dinners, recognition in company publications
- better office space, equipment, or furnishings; preferred parking spaces
- cash awards, gift certificates, merchandise awards, gold coins, travel
- conferences, training, and professional development opportunities
- outstanding employee awards, salary and benefits increases, stock options
- promotion, enjoyable responsibilities, choice of projects, more autonomy

Your college or university is not structured to provide many of the rewards listed above. If you search your memory and your campus publications, however, you may be surprised at the various rewards students receive for academic and co-curricular achievements. Identify the most common rewards below. While you are at it, also identify some of the punishments that your institution administers to change student behavior.

_____

_____

_____

Now identify those rewards (intrinsic and extrinsic) and punishments that most strongly influence *your* motivation and behavior.

_____

_____

_____

Whether or not we like to admit it, these factors can serve as powerful motivators of our beliefs and behaviors.

Observational Learning

Observational learning or modeling is learning by observing or imitating the behavior or beliefs of others. The process sometimes occurs so quickly that we are unaware that it is happening (e.g., a classmate shows you how to archive an e-mail message), or the behavior is acquired but not performed until a later time (e.g., using the Heimlich maneuver you saw demonstrated in a first aid class). Like operant learning, modeling is pervasive from infancy onward, especially in the acquisition of social behaviors. Observational learning informs students and employees about how to perform specific tasks or procedures, what to say (or not say), what to wear and on what days, who to associate or not associate with, how to respond to particular individuals, and numerous other situations. In the larger perspective, observational learning simultaneously reflects and molds an organization's climate, culture, and traditions. Even the nonconformist pays attention to others' actions, to learn what not to do. But do people really learn that much from imitation? Take a few minutes and list 10 activities or "things" you do (or avoid doing) on a regular basis that were at least partially learned by imitating someone or something. Don't hesitate to include activities that are part of your college or workplace traditions, as well as individual behaviors you have observed in the classroom, residence halls, and other venues.

_____	_____
_____	_____
_____	_____
_____	_____
_____	_____

FROM INTUIT TO DO IT: THE EXPERIENTIAL LEARNING CYCLE

Operant and observational learning principles account for changes in specific behaviors and beliefs, but they do not explain the *strategies* people often follow when they face new situations. When you begin a new job, transfer to a new college, assemble a piece of furniture, visit a foreign country, or begin a new hobby or sport, what steps, plan, or strategy do you follow to understand and deal with the situation? Kolb et al. (1995) believe that learning follows a four-stage cycle that is diagrammed in Figure 6.1. As we summarize this model, choose one of the previous examples or one of your own and imagine how you would proceed in that situation.

According to Kolb, learning begins by experiencing a situation concretely and directly (concrete experiences) as it is, intuitively, whether it is the first two days of a new job, at college, in Spain, in the gym, or your first encounter with that unassembled computer desk. You subsequently observe and reflect on your experiences, comparing your expectations and past experiences (e.g., with other jobs, colleges, travel, or furniture assembly) to the new situation or reflecting on your feelings and attitudes toward the new experience. In the third stage you interpret the meaning of your experiences (e.g., Was it satisfying or frustrating? How could I do it better?) and create a generalization or hypothesis about how to proceed (e.g., "stay the course," make changes, get help). In the final stage, you test your new hypotheses and generalizations and proceed, a process that often leads to repetition of the learning cycle. In similar situations (a new job, college, country, or assembling furniture) you will repeat the cycle, modify concepts where appropriate, and apply what you learned in past situations to your new experience. Learning involves the continuous

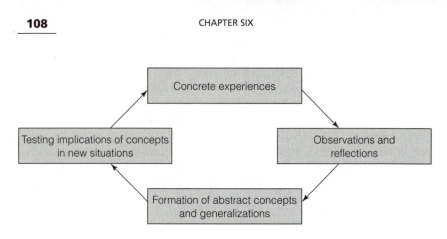

FIGURE 6.1 Kolb's experiential learning cycle

SOURCE: From *Organizational behavior: An experiential approach* (6th ed.), (p. 49), by Kolb, D. A., Osland J. S., and Rubin, I. M. 1995, Englewood Cliffs, NJ: Prentice-Hall. Reprinted with permission of Pearson Education, Inc.

repetition of the cycle: experiencing, reflecting, forming hypotheses, and testing hypotheses. You have encountered this process several times in the past, especially in your science courses.

"Interesting," you say, "but what does this have to do with college and career?" As a result of repeating the experiential learning cycle countless times in your life, you may have developed a preference or disdain for one stage or another. Kolb regards the four stages as orientations, modes of learning, or learning preferences. Persons who have learned (perhaps through reinforcement and imitation) to prefer the *concrete experiences* orientation are likely to rely on feelings, hunches, intuition, and direct experience (versus the formation of abstract concepts) as they immerse themselves in the immediate experience of new situations. They are open to new experiences, work well in unstructured situations, and are people-oriented. Individuals who prefer the *observation and reflections* mode are likely to be detached observers who seek to comprehend the dimensions of the problem from afar rather than become actively involved. They tend to prefer to approach new situations with patience, thoughtfulness, and multiple perspectives rather than jumping in. Persons oriented to the *formation of abstract concepts and generalizations* often prefer to use logic, analysis, and reasoning when confronted with new situations rather than trust immediate experience. They are likely to use a planned, methodical, and rigorous approach to solving problems. Finally, those who prefer the immediate, practical, "hands-on" approach (versus reflection) to dealing with new situations prefer *testing implications* of concepts in new situations. The orientations of concrete experience and formation of abstract concepts are somewhat opposite of each other; observations and reflection and testing implications are also opposites. Kolb developed a paper-and-pencil scale called the Learning Styles Inventory that combines scores representing the four orientations into various learning styles. The exposition of these learning styles is beyond the goals of this chapter, but Kolb's scale is one of several measures of learning styles that some counselors and instructors use to illustrate learning. In essence, Kolb believes that learning is the differential use of the four learning orientations to interpret our experiences and use them to deal with future situations. (Kolb et al., 1995)

Do you have a learning orientation that you prefer or one that you avoid? Have you ever considered that your successes or difficulties with certain courses or instructors may be due, at least in part, to the relationship between your preferred modes of learning and the instructor's preferred methods of presenting material and assignments? Svinicki and Dixon (1987) believe that some instructional approaches favor certain orientations to learning, as represented in the examples they provide below. As you reflect on each instructional approach, perhaps you can associate it generally with particular skills, jobs, or careers.

Concrete experiences: laboratory or fieldwork, problems, examples, data collection, simulations, interviews

Observation and reflections: journals, discussion, thought questions

Formation of abstract concepts and generalizations: lectures, papers, projects, model building

Testing implications of concepts in new situations: projects, simulations, case studies, field and homework

As Kolb regards all four stages essential to learning, students should take courses that collectively support all modes. For example, if you are weak in observing and reflecting, regard journal writing (our Journal Starters), class discussions, or thought questions as a positive challenge to strengthen this mode of learning. If concrete experiences or testing implications is your strong area, then be open to careers where you can use those strengths, but be sure to take courses where other stages in the process are emphasized. Finally, remember that typical college courses are characterized by the second and third stages (quintessential thinking skills). Yet in numerous entry-level positions, your tasks will allow little time to reflect, and analytical reasoning and logic will not be rewarded consistently. Recall from the taxonomy of new employee learning tasks (chapter 2) its emphasis on individual, interpersonal, and organizational dimensions. Also, chapter 5 addressed the role of analytical thinking within the broad scope of intelligence and intelligent behavior.

Gaining skills in Kolb's four modes of learning is not limited to the classroom; consider other venues of college life where orientations to learning can be tested and strengthened.

- Search for leadership opportunities in student government, clubs, residence halls, student life, and academic departments that can develop all or most of Kolb's four orientations.

- Service learning, internships, and certain independent studies can emphasize any one or a combination of the four stages.

- While some jobs are truly mundane, almost any job can be educational if you work at it. Gather feedback from your job about your most- and least-preferred modes of learning; your supervisor and co-workers likely serve as positive or negative role models.

Knowing your most- and least-preferred learning orientations can be cues to coursework, instructors, part-time jobs, and careers. As indicated in chapter 2, the world of work is different from the structured, repetitive 15–17 years in the educational workplace where learning is measured by paper-and-pencil exams. How often have you seen job descriptions that require experience in taking multiple-choice tests? Some jobs require report writing (analogous to term papers), but seldom do you have the time to write an excellent report, as you did in college. Few if any jobs require long reading periods in preparation for lectures. *Learning is mostly learning by doing.* Learning and job performance may be one and the same, as Nancy Dixon indicates in a quotation that opened this chapter. Shoshana Zuboff expands on this point (Dixon 1999).

> Learning is no longer a separate activity that occurs either before one enters the workplace or in remote classroom settings. . . . The behaviors that define learning and the behaviors that define being productive are one and the same. Learning is not something that requires time out from being engaged in productive activity; learning is the heart of productive activity. *To put it simply, learning is the new form of labor* (p. 395, emphasis added).

SUMMING UP

Your primary reason for achieving a college degree is to prepare for a personal and professional future that enables you to fulfill your dreams. Motives are the energizing force, the work clothes, of your dreams. During college, you shift your motivational energy from predominantly external to predominantly internal sources. Motives are influenced by several factors, including your goals, your relationships with peers and supervisors, and your beliefs about effort and its outcomes. Although college has taught you strategies for thinking and problem solving, performance in college and corporate workplaces is also heavily influenced by operant and observational learning. The experiential model of learning asserts that you develop preferred modes of learning (learning styles) in response to new situations. Consequently you seek opportunities during college that help you strengthen all modes of learning; you will need the flexibility to shift from one mode to another when needed. Most of all, remember that motivation and learning can be elusive processes. Sometimes you are their master; other times you are convinced you have neither the energy, direction, nor tools to get where you want to be, wherever that is. Although some students know (or think they know) exactly what they want to do in life, for most students the road to the future consists of hills, curves, and detours. Case in Point 6.1 presents three scenarios depicting students whose paths took significant detours from their original starting points.

CASE IN POINT 6.1   The Zig-Zag Road to the Future

Life is a continuous journey. Learning is the vehicle that carries us, and motivation provides the fuel and direction. Seldom is the road straight, and a road that zig-zags becomes the impetus for real change.

Phil didn't want to go to college. When his parents gave him the ultimatum of attending college or getting a job and becoming self-sufficient, however, he chose school. He got by in his coursework during the first two years, but was not excited about his experiences, including his communications major. Late in his sophomore year, he enrolled in a theater participation course and enjoyed it so much he declared a double major in theatre and communications. He enjoyed the intense "hands-on" nature of technical theatre, the close comraderie of theater students, his demanding but excellent teachers, and the artistic and intellectual challenges theatre provided. Theatre also connected to his high school "garage band" experiences and his parents' enjoyment of the arts. After graduation, to everyone's surprise, he entered a graduate theatre program, earned a master's degree, completed teacher certification requirements, and subsequently taught technical theatre in high school where he also found good use for his communications major. During his junior year of college he had joined the U.S. Army Reserves and received training in leadership and teamwork, Signal Corps (communications), Psychological Operations, and other areas. The experiences he gained in his band, combined with his college theatre experiences, were used in the coordinating and development of a highly sophistical mobile communications system used by the military. Like many men and women who joined the active-duty military or reserves, he was deployed to Iraq during the war in 2003 and served as a Civil Affairs officer. Phil would never have imagined, as a college sophomore uncertain about his academic major or future, the numerous diverse and meaningful experiences that subsequently shaped his life.

Miharu studied sociology with the goal of becoming a social worker because she wanted to be in a profession that helps people. During her junior year, however, as she learned more about the field, the importance of obtaining a graduate degree, and the challenges social work poses, she began to question her confidence and ability to work in that profession. She accepted a summer clerical job in the human resources office of a nearby medium-size corporation where she saw peers and supervisors helping employees with insurance and benefits plans, retirement issues, and personal problems. She liked what she saw and wanted to switch her major to business, but as a senior she knew she was too close to graduation to change. Instead she used her senior year electives to complete courses in economics, management, computer software, and human resources management. Along with her sociology major, these courses and summer experiences were sufficient to land her an entry-level position in the human resources department of an area corporation.

From high school on, Rebecca enjoyed art and psychology, so she declared a double major in these disciplines during her sophomore year of college. Along the way, she completed an art therapy course and

(Continued)

CASE IN POINT 6.1   Continued

a practicum. She thought that she would like to obtain a master's degree in art therapy, but was never enthusiastic about it. During the summer between her junior and senior years, she completed courses in statistics and research methods, requirements for her major. To her great surprise, she enjoyed them very much. Rebecca, now a senior, was in a quandary: She enjoyed art and psychology, but she did not want to commit to a career in art therapy. What should she do about her new interest in research? She jumped at an opportunity her advisor offered to complete a research internship at a nearby medical school. Rebecca thoroughly enjoyed the research, her mentor, and the weekly graduate student research discussions she was permitted to attend. When the professional association held their annual meeting nearby, she was excited to hear and meet researchers whose work she had read. She subsequently applied to graduate school in health psychology, with the goal of teaching, conducting research, and possibly incorporating her art background into her work.

For all of these students, the road followed took a sharp turn during their last years of college in ways each would not have predicted as freshmen or sophomores. They took risks. They could have remained comfortable in

the majors they had first chosen and could have completed them successfully. However, they were dissatisfied with current choices, open to change, and valued new opportunities and the rewards they offered. Their experiences guided their motivational and learning processes thoughtfully down other roads, roads that may continue to zig and zag.

Reread these scenarios and try to answer the following questions using the information given.

1. Were the changes that each student made powered mainly by intrinsic or extrinsic motivation?
2. To what extent could goal setting, expectancy theory, or equity theory play a role in the experiences of each?
3. What roles could operant and observational learning play at particular points for each person?
4. Although their stories are brief, what roles could their orientations or modes of learning occupy in their decisions?

"We make progress by a constant spiraling back and forth between the inner world and the outer one, the personal and the political, the self and the circumstances. Nature doesn't move in a straight line, and as part of nature, neither do we." Gloria Steinem

JOURNAL STARTERS

1. Which motivational concepts best describe your motivation: (a) as a first-year student, and (b) now? Which concepts are most likely to influence your motivation in your first job after college?

2. Write a list of five to seven specific activities or behaviors that you performed today. For each, try to determine the extent to which it was

influenced by operant or observational learning or by the experiential learning cycle.

3. What are the features or characteristics of the classes and teachers of your most and least preferred courses? To what extent do any of the concepts presented in this chapter (especially Kolb's learning cycle) explain your thoughts and feelings about these courses?

4. Using the three components of goal-setting theory, state at least two realistic academic short-term (within next six to twelve months), intermediate (one to three years), and two long-term (four to six years) professional goals you wish to accomplish. Do the same for at least two of your personal goals.

5. What are the two or three most significant insights you acquired from reading this material? What ideas or issues concern you most?

FYI

www.SIOP.org—the website for the Society of Industrial and Organizational Psychology, a division of the American Psychological Association

www.myGoals.com—provides information that shows you how to establish and monitor personal and professional goals.

REFERENCES

Baxter Magolda, M. B. (1996). Post-college experiences and epistemology. *The Review of Higher Education.* 18(1): 25–44.

Dixon, N. M. (1999). The Organizational Learning Cycle: How We Can Learn Collectively. Aldenshot, Hampshire, England: Gowe Publishing Limited.

Donovan, J. J. (2001). Work motivation. In N. Anderson, D. S. Ones, H. K. Sinangil, and C. Viswesvaran (Eds.), *Handbook of industrial, work and organizational psychology.* Volume II, (pp 53–76). London: Sage.

Gardner, P. D. (1998). Are college seniors prepared to work? In J. N. Gardner, G. Van der Veer, & Associates. *The senior year experience: Facilitating integration, reflection, closure, and transition.* San Francisco, CA: Jossey-Bass Publishers.

Greenberg, J., and Baron, R. A. (2000). *Behavior in organizations* (7th ed). Upper Saddle River, NJ: Prentice-Hall.

Halonen, J. S., & Santrock, J. W. (1996). *Psychology: Contexts of behavior.* Chicago, IL: Brown & Benchmark.

Holton, E. F. III (1998). Preparing students for life beyond the classroom. In J. Gardner, G. Van der Veer, & Associates. *The senior year experience: Facilitating integration, reflection, closure, and transition.* San Francisco, CA: Jossey-Bass.

Kim, W. C., & Mauborgne, R. (2003). Fair process: Managing in the knowledge economy. *Harvard Business Review.* 81(1): 127–136.

Kolb, D.A., Osland, J. S., and Rubin, I. M. (1995). *Organizational behavior: An Experiential approach* (6th ed.). Englewood Cliffs, NJ: Prentice-Hall.

Nelson, B. (1994). *1001 ways to reward employees.* New York, NY: Workman Publishing Co.

Svinicki, M. D., and Dixon, N. M. (1987). The Kolb model modified for classroom activities. *College Teaching.* 35(4): 141–146.

7

Relationships— at Home, at Work, in the Community

When the gusty winds blow and shake our lives, if we know that people care about us, we may bend with the wind . . . but we won't break.

FRED ROGERS (2003)

It is likely that you spent a part of your childhood watching *Sesame Street* and *Mr. Rogers Neighborhood*. Each of these shows, in its own particular way, conveyed a sense of belonging—a sense of community. It was this sense of *belongingness*, perhaps more than any of the characters or familiar topics, that resonated with young viewers. Mr. Rogers welcomed all of us to his neighborhood. Everyone could get to *Sesame Street*. They were places where you were happy to meet your neighbors, and they were pleased to meet you.

You probably came to college from your own neighborhood—a place where you knew everyone on your block. You usually ran into someone you knew when you were at the mall or in the library. Perhaps you went to kindergarten with the same kids who populated your high school graduation class. You may have worshipped together at the same church, played together on the same Little League and soccer teams, and been frightened together by the same scary stories during a weekend camping trip with the Scouts. As a matter of fact, one of the most appealing things about going to college is that it provides an escape from all this "togetherness."

A HOME AWAY FROM HOME

College gives most freshmen the opportunity to re-invent themselves; and they do so several times in the course of their academic careers. It is interesting, however, that the first thing most freshmen do is to look for a place to belong. They make immediate connections with roommates or suitemates. They join a fraternity or sorority, an intramural team, hall government, the student newspaper. They find clubs and organizations that reflect their cultural, racial, or religious traditions. They find an on-campus job. In short, they re-create their neighborhood in their collegiate environment.

At about the junior year, these connections begin to loosen a bit. Students move off campus to apartments or houses. While they are often thrilled to have their own places, they also leave behind the potential connections they can make in a residence hall setting. Internships and jobs off campus are more common during the last two years of college. These students need both broader exposure to prepare for their careers and money for those extra bills that an apartment can generate. The time that was once available for clubs and teams is now much more limited.

Coursework is more challenging as well. The days of intro classes and 150-person lecture halls have given way to smaller, 300-level classes. During their junior and senior years, students are focused on completing the requirements for their majors, and they are doing so with other students who are in the same major. While this is an exciting period intellectually, it limits the opportunities to branch out and meet new people. This is also the time when students may elect to study abroad. A semester or full academic year in a foreign country can be an eye-opening experience; once they return to campus, however, students are often unable to maintain the communities they created overseas. It seems apparent that, while college life begins broadly, it narrows over time. The limits that appear are based upon each person's professional goals, personal responsibilities, and the distillation of their interests. By graduation the neighborhood has gotten smaller and, perhaps, more impersonal. In some cases it seems to have disappeared, and nothing points to an obvious replacement for this lost sense of community and belonging.

This chapter focuses on your relationships with other people—your friends, your family, your work groups, your mentors, your community—and the changes that are waiting for you or the changes that you are currently experiencing. The first goal of this chapter is to identify the relational changes that are inherent in the passage from college to career and concomitant shifts in behavior that may be helpful to you. In short, it alerts you to what to expect and how to approach it. You are not alone if you are struggling with relationship issues. Apparently, it is a very well kept secret that loneliness, balancing work commitments and personal relationships, and understanding the demands of work groups are practically universal issues for young adults. Finally, this chapter offers some ideas and processes that will not provide immediate relief, but will, over time, help you improve the quality of your interactions and build or restore satisfying, meaningful relationships in your personal and professional life.

THE SHIFTING SANDS
OF PERSONAL RELATIONSHIPS

Songwriters often have a wonderful and romantic, if somewhat unrealistic, sense of friendship and kinship. Simon and Garfunkel promised to "bridge troubled water," while James Taylor and Carole King swore that they would "come running" to you if you called their name. However, in today's world of long hours, limited time off, corporate travel, and intense competition, the friend or relative you need might be at a sales meeting in Buffalo, holed up in a law library researching a case that goes to court in a couple of days, or sleeping at work to monitor the IT upgrade that's being installed overnight. Whether friends and family live cross-town or across the country, keeping connected can be tough.

Keeping Friendships Alive and Well

The book *Quarterlife Crisis* suggests that the drastic change in social life after graduation is a major cause of depression among twentysomethings (Robbins and Wilner 2001). Many variables increase the level of difficulty required to keep current friendships strong. Many young adults find it necessary to move away from their friends. They take a job in another state. They decide to live at home for a while. While a new job in a new place can be exciting, and living with the folks is certainly cheap, foregoing easy and immediate access to friends is a huge loss. Meet Robyn (Case in Point 7.1). Her story illustrates many of these points.

Robbins and Wilner's (2001) findings reinforces the notion that Robyn's experience is all too common. They suggest that new graduates are not shocked by the fact that maintaining a quality social life is a chore. "What is harder for them to figure out is how to meet people after school, how much time and energy to put into meeting those people, and what to do once they have already met them—keeping in mind, among other things, their financial, geographical, and time constraints" (p. 181).

When we asked Robyn if we could use her story, she consented whole-heartedly. She spent a great deal of time discussing "if there is life after college" with her friends and siblings and recognizes that her experience is not unique to people who enter nursing. She realizes that it's important to know that "you're not the only one going through it."

It's All in the Family

Changes in family relationships are also a part of the adjustment faced by young adults, both before and after graduation. Throughout college, students must negotiate with their families around career choices, living arrangements, financial support, and general acceptance and approval. College graduation

CASE IN POINT 7.1   Robyn's True Life Adventure

In Robyn's last year of college, her nursing major required her to spend more time in hospitals completing her clinical rotations than on campus. In fact, six weeks of her final semester were spent in London, where she took the opportunity to do a community nursing rotation and experience life in the UK. When she returned to school, it was to the hospital, not the classroom. While she rarely made it to campus anymore, she still had as much social interaction (mostly with the other senior nursing students) as her schedule would allow.

After graduation Robyn moved out of her apartment, which was located a few blocks from campus, and into her parents' basement. She was now about 40 miles from the major midwestern city that was her home during college. During the first few months, Robyn focused on studying for the Nursing Boards. She took the Boards in July and three weeks later received the happy news that she had passed. Because she excelled clinically, she received several job offers; however, she decided to stay in the hospital that had employed her for the last 18 months. By mid-August, she was working at least 40 hours a week on the evening shift, with two hours a day added by her commute. She had reached the goal she had worked so hard to achieve. She was a registered nurse on a medical-surgical unit of a major metropolitan medical center. She was also lonely and miserable.

Because Robyn worked evenings and every other weekend, she found it almost impossible to connect with her friends—many of whom were nurses with opposite schedules. Her lengthy commute (an 80 mile round trip) became the bane of her existence. On the days she was off, she wasn't anxious to take the ride back into the city to meet up with her friends. She succinctly described her life as "Get up . . . work . . . come home . . . sleep . . . do it all over again."

Robyn made several major changes that improved her ability to connect with her friends. While her initial intention was to live with her family until she paid off her bills and had saved some money, she decided to move back into the city after three months of full-time employment. She rented a studio apartment within walking distance of her hospital. While her move solved one problem, it created another. Robyn had never lived alone before and discovered that she didn't like it much. Since a roommate wasn't an option, Robyn got a cat. Frankie (the cat) wasn't big on conversation, but he was happy to see her.

Are we at the happy ending part yet? Unfortunately, no. Robyn still had to deal with the fact that nursing schedules don't allow for "typical" social lives. She discovered that she had to make an extra effort to stay connected to friends. A spontaneous social life like the one she led in college was not an option anymore. Being with her friends now meant planning ahead. She also had to make decisions to work out or go shopping when she had the time vs. when other people might be available.

After her first year as a nurse, Robyn was able to switch to the day shift. While her weekends are not always free, her evenings are. This final change has made her feel as though she not only has more time, but also more control over the time she has available. The first year was a tough one for Robyn, with more adjustments than she had anticipated. She had worked since she was in high school, but had never experienced the

CASE IN POINT 7.1   Continued

effects of a full-time job. She came from a big family, where being alone was often a luxury. However, living alone was a very different experience. She had not factored in the toll that commuting would take on her because she had never had a long, daily commute before. She made friends easily and always had a very active social life. It never occurred to her that maintaining friendships would take so much work or that meeting new people would seem almost impossible at times.

doesn't necessarily change the need for accountability or support of one kind or another. Of course, different families have different levels of involvement. The challenge of graduation and young adulthood is the re-negotiation of boundaries, especially for those college grads who have returned to live with their families.

The research of Csikszentmihalyi and Schneider (2000) . . . offers "concrete evidence that families matter in an adolescent's career development" (p. 228). They go on to say that love and support must be coupled with opportunities for responsible behavior, recognition of accomplishments, and high expectations. Parental responsibilities include learning about adolescents' talents and interests and channeling them into real life experiences. While this hands-on approach is recommended through college, what is appropriate after graduation?

Andrea, a college graduate interviewed for *Quarterlife Crisis,* acknowledges her need for her parents' approval.

> Some people, I think would suggest that . . . if I were 'really' an adult, I would be able to discover what I 'really think' is right, apart from the influence of my parents. The problem with these people's understanding of freedom is that when what I 'really think'—which more often that not, means what immediately strikes me as comfortable—trumps everything else, I'm doomed to live in a world no bigger than my own whims . . . . I think that parents—and family in general—provide one's means to true freedom. If I concede that there are some cases in which my parents may know better than I do, then I'm placing myself in a world and a story that's much bigger than myself (Robbins and Wilner 2001, p. 56).

Andrea is choosing to enlist the counsel of her parents. They have the role of trusted advisors—people who can mentor her emerging adulthood. Their relationship may be the best of all possible worlds.

Other young adults make the move home and have difficulty adjusting to their parents' rules and/or opinions regarding their social life or spending habits. Many parents feel that they still have a responsibility to offer input, with or without being asked. Parents, too, have become accustomed to a way of life that hasn't needed to take their returning son or daughter into consideration. In the end, most families make compromises that allow a peace, or at least a truce, to exist until their new grads get on their feet occupationally and financially.

Some grads discover that the only way to move into adulthood, however, is to build a nest of their own. In *Quarterlife Crisis,* Devon, a new grad, says, "This is definitely a transition time and this is how I feel I need to make my transition: by becoming fully self supportive financially, emotionally, physically, and spiritually. I personally didn't feel that I could do that under my parents' roof" (Robbins and Wilner 2001, pp. 58–59).

For the young adults who find themselves far away from family, the adjustments are different in some respects. While geography determines some obvious, and perhaps, welcome boundaries, it also creates some significant roadblocks to maintaining family relationships. Young adults worry about remaining connected to siblings, nieces and nephews, grandparents. That they are not around for many family events is often the cause of disappointment and loneliness. Finding ways to connect during this critical time of transition is imperative. Technology can be an extremely helpful tool in maintaining ties. Cell phones (with no extra charges for long distance), calling cards, and e-mail can be important and cost-effective links. The key, during college and afterward, is to let your family know what you need. Then, together, you can decide how your needs will get met.

RELATIONSHIPS AT WORK

There you are on your first day at your new job—a brand new college graduate ready to take on the world. Perhaps a little anxious, perhaps a little scared, but, nonetheless, you are ready. You arrive at your new workplace, walk inside, and suddenly you feel like Dorothy. The doors of Oz have just opened, and it looks and feels nothing like anything you have ever experienced before. You don't know how things work here. You don't know what the rules are, and you don't know whom to ask. Chances are that you have the skills to do the actual work, but managing in the environment is a complete mystery to you. While new employee orientations certainly provide some of the information you will need to master the work environment, much of the help you need can't be found in a presentation, a textbook, or on-line.

Chapter 2 discusses relationships as one of Holton's categories of new employee learning tasks. How you can meet your colleagues, establish a good rapport and effective working relationships, and find the support you need to do your job are major questions for every new grad—questions to which there are some answers.

Help Is on the Way

Meeting the people in your work group—as soon as you hang up your coat, if possible—is the first important step to learning how things work. In the beginning it is important that you spend more time listening to and observing your colleagues than "chatting them up." What are you listening for?

Co-Worker's Names Work hard to remember them. The easiest way to start out on solid footing is to use people's names when speaking with them. Never assume that you can use a nickname. If you were introduced to Kenneth, shortening his name to Ken (without being told it is an option) is not likely to score any points. If Kenneth has told you about people or things that are important to him (including the names of his kids or his dog), try to remember those names as well. It gives you a way to connect on a daily basis that demonstrates your interest but is not overly personal.

What Do People Really Do? This information is rarely contained in a job title. What are their actual responsibilities—what are their areas of expertise—what are their interests both on and off the job? Your office manager may also administer the budget (always good to know who is in charge of the money), recognize every person in the organization, know whom to call to circumvent the red tape involved in fixing your computer when it crashes or where to order food for a last minute meeting, and be an amazing graphic designer (see last year's department Christmas card).

How Are People Supposed to Behave? What does "business casual" really mean? How is time spent at the office—flexible as long as you get your work done or is there an "on-time is late" philosophy? How does lunch work— do people bring their lunch and eat together in the cafeteria, order in during meetings or busy days so they can continue to work while they eat, always take a break, etc.? Do people do things together after work, on the weekends—is there a softball team, bowling league, running group that meets weekly, picnic in the summer, ski trip in the winter?

What's the Communication Protocol? What are the standards for interoffice communication? Are "hallway meetings" the norm? Are there weekly (or bi-weekly) staff meetings and how are people prepared for them? Is e-mail typically sent to the entire office group or routed from individual-to-individual? How strong is the grapevine and is it accurate? How is conflict handled between colleagues?

Who Knows the Scoop? Who has the answers you need? Who communicates directly and fairly? Who offers assistance graciously and supportively? Who understands the organizational network and is well-connected? Who is always tapped into the grapevine? Who is willing to help without the need to "recruit" you into a particular brand of office politics?

The knowledge that you can pick up in the first few weeks by simply opening your eyes and ears is amazing and crucial to your understanding of how work works! Armed with this information, it is easier (although not foolproof) to operate effectively in the work environment. There will be times when you will feel the need to change or even disregard the norms; but before you do that, you need to know what the rules are and why they are structured in a particular way.

Playing Well with Others

And no matter what happens—injury, sitting on the bench for foul language, harassing the coach, etc. Good hits, bad hits, no hits, good days, off days, playing your best, not playing your best. In the end, if the team does its job, everyone goes to the World Series, everyone gets a ring and everyone is a champion.

Babe Ruth

You probably played on some kind of team at some point in your life and remember what it felt like to win—especially if you were the one who scored in the last seconds of the game or performed better than you ever had. On the other hand, you probably also remember what it felt like to miss a shot, to strike out, to hit a wrong note and, in the end, to blame yourself for the loss or the less-than-perfect performance. Either way, some adult—a coach or a parent—told you that you couldn't take all the credit or all the blame. You win and lose as a team.

In college, you have participated in study groups, made group presentations, and worked on group projects and papers. Your volunteer experiences, community service work, internships, fieldwork, nursing rotations, student teaching, etc. not only taught you the skills of your discipline, but also provided you with many opportunities to both witness and work with a team. Certainly your involvement in residence life, the school paper, the campus radio station, student government, ministry immersion trips, or any student group honed your team skills. Csikszentmihalyi and Schneider (2000) maintain that the group work you have done in school is excellent preparation for the teamwork that will now be required. "Whereas students find teachers' lectures boring, they find group work engaging and challenging, and group work is what employers want workers to be able to do" (p. 232).

Once again you find yourself on a team. As a matter of fact, it is sometimes difficult to recognize where your job begins and someone else's ends; in some respects, it doesn't matter. What does matter is that for the team to be successful each member has to do his/her part. On one hand you have spent a good deal of your educational life in work groups. On the other hand, since most employers list the ability to work as an effective member of a team as one of the top skills they seek in new hires, your job may depend on your ability to be a good team player, perhaps more than any other talent you possess. Given the high stakes nature of the team you are now a part of, it is important to understand the factors that make teams and team members successful.

Greenberg and Baron (2000) define *team* as "a group whose members have complementary skills and are committed to a common purpose or set of performance goals for which they hold themselves mutually accountable" (p. 271). Successful teams, according to Greenberg and Baron (2000):

- have members with diverse skill sets and experiences that will be useful to the purpose and performance of the team

- are compact, using the smallest number of people necessary to do the work
- are trained and cross-trained in the technical skills necessary to reach their goals and in the team interaction skills necessary to work well together
- have a well-defined mission and clearly articulated goals
- develop and evaluate their own performance expectations
- acknowledge and reward members for key contributions to the achievement of team goals
- promote clear, respectful communication among members
- encourage dissenting voices and differing opinions
- manage conflicts and issues constructively, directly, and immediately
- foster participation, cooperation, trust and team spirit
- seek out and remain open to new information
- keep connected to the larger organization, sharing progress and soliciting feedback

It is not likely that your work group will have all the hallmarks of a highly effective team, but hopefully you will see some similarities. It is also important to recognize your role in the team. Are you communicating effectively? Helping other team members in need? Recognizing others' efforts and contributions? Managing disagreements appropriately? The following questionnaire will assist you in assessing your skills as a team member.

Are You a Team Player?

1. Read each of the following statements and carefully consider whether it accurately describes your team membership style (most of the time).
2. On the line next to each statement, write "Yes" if the statement is typical of you and "No" if it is not. If you are uncertain, write a question mark ("?").

Most of the time, when I am working with a team, I . . .

1. _____ Am ethical in my approach to tasks and problem-solving.
2. _____ Keep my commitments.
3. _____ Recognize and respond to needs without being asked.
4. _____ Maintain the rules and practices of the group.
5. _____ Make team goals my priority.
6. _____ Am willing to help other group members learn new skills.
7. _____ Complete tasks in keeping with quality and efficiency standards.
8. _____ Am cooperative and willing to coordinate my work with others.

9. _____ Attend all meetings on time and am prepared to work.

10. _____ Note nonverbal as well as verbal cues and respond appropriately.

11. _____ Share any new information that has come to my attention.

12. _____ Ask questions and encourage others to do the same.

13. _____ Recognize the positive ideas of others.

14. _____ Listen attentively.

15. _____ Affirm the contributions of others.

16. _____ Offer constructive feedback.

17. _____ Welcome others' constructive feedback.

18. _____ Communicate ideas clearly and non-judgmentally.

19. _____ Disagree in a timely and tactful manner.

20. _____ Am open to others' opinions and willing to change my mind.

Things to Consider . . .

- List the teams on which you have worked and played while in college. Remember to include study, volunteer, and church groups as well as athletic teams and student organizations.

  _____

  _____

  _____

- What are the team skills in which you excel? How can you help other team members develop these skills?

  _____

  _____

- Which of your team skills require development? What steps will you take to improve these skills? What is your timeline for change?

  _____

  _____

  _____

SOURCE: *Behavior in Organizations.* 7 ed by Greenberg and Baron © (2000). Adapted by permission of Pearson Education, Inc., Upper Saddle River, NJ.

Unfortunately many teams fail to achieve their goals. One look at the list of attributes of an effective team suggests how easy it would be to miss the mark. There are particular problems that are almost always lethal to team achievement, as the story in Case in Point 7.2 illustrates.

CASE IN POINT 7.2   The Strategic Planning Committee

Several years ago the authors of this book served on a Strategic Planning Committee of a small liberal arts college. The college was faced with severe financial problems, dwindling enrollments, and poor employee morale. Our charge was to recommend changes that would reflect the college's mission while increasing income and enrollments and decreasing spending. The team, consisting of 15–20 people from all areas of the college, worked for months on this plan. We worked nights, weekends, through holidays and breaks. We developed a respect for each other and felt strongly about our role in saving the institution. We gathered input from the academic, administrative, and student services divisions, but didn't offer these areas much information on our direction or progress. We slowly and thoroughly crafted our proposal; if there were dissenting opinions among us, they weren't given much credence.

Much to our surprise, the rest of the college was not anywhere near as enthusiastic as we were about the work we were trying to accomplish. The committee viewed the lack of support as fear of change and refusal to make the "paradigm shift" necessary to keep the college going. Truth be told, we felt very unappreciated; but, since the fate of the college was in our hands, it was imperative that we achieve our goals regardless of the undercurrent of dissent that was clearly ready to surface.

Finally, at a meeting that was attended by most of the faculty, staff, and administrators, the strategic plan was unveiled. The next sounds heard were those of the plan as it crashed and burned. The audience hated the plan, and they weren't too keen on its creators. One of the last people to speak out against the plan was a senior faculty member. She said that she had passed a church on her way to the college that day and thought that the "quote of the day" on the church's sign said it all. The sign read, "God so loved the world that He did not send a committee."

The postscript to this situation was that, while the college indeed survived, it did so without using the majority of the Strategic Planning Committee's recommendations. The institution did implement one or two of the more modest ideas, but the plans for sweeping change went largely ignored.

- Using the list of attributes of a successful team, identify what went wrong with the Strategic Planning Committee.

  _____

  _____

  _____

- Make recommendations that would have helped this team achieve its goals.

  _____

  _____

  _____

THE IMPORTANCE OF MENTORS

An option to consider when trying to participate in a community, understand the organizational culture, or enhance your professional skill set is to look for role models to mentor your personal and career development. There are enormous benefits to being mentored, not the least of which is the support necessary to help you develop confidence and distinguish opportunities. Some mentoring relationships are brief encounters and some are the long-term result of a complex selection process. Either way you can only profit from the mentors in your life.

Mentors for Your Career

In their book *Common Fire,* L. Parks Daloz, C. H. Keen, J. P. Keen, and S. Daloz Parks (1996) point to the importance of mentors during the transition from school to work. They maintain that ". . . young adults need mentors and mentoring environments to usher them into the world of adult work. College may be an initial mentoring environment, but graduation can be a critical juncture. A job? Graduate or professional school? Travel? The choices are life-determining" (p. 48). One of the young adults they interviewed elaborated on the value of a mentor to interns as well as new employees.

> What these mentors do, see, is teach you the rules. The rules aren't written anywhere; you can't go buy a book. It's from my mouth to your ears and you have to continue to pass it along that way . . . That's my responsibility to make it a little easier for them (the new interns). Because I was the first one to hire on, I told them what the hiring process is like, how to negotiate the salaries, and little things to look out for. Because someone's done it for me, I've got to do it for someone else . . . It's invaluable knowledge . . . (p. 101).

In more formal mentoring arrangements, there are four distinct phases that the relationship passes through. In the *initiation* phase, you are getting to know your mentor. You are both learning what each of you has to offer and what you can expect from each other. The *cultivation* phase may last several years and is typified by rapid career progress as a result of the mentor's help. In the *separation* phase, you may feel the need to "fly solo." You are ready and anxious to operate independently. The final phase is *redefinition*. The relationship changes and, typically, friendship and equality emerge (Greenberg and Baron 2000).

While career mentors are often found within the work place, it is also possible to connect with mentors through professional associations, your alumni association, your church, fraternities and sororities, etc. The key is to look around and find people whose work you respect and whose skills you want to emulate. Search for ". . . somebody that will take time to guide you along, and somebody that's recognized as being a leader in their profession" (Csikszentmihalyi 2003, p. 175).

Mentors for Life

Mentors challenge, support, and inspire . . . They function as compelling women and men who recognize and support the emerging competence of the young adult, challenge limited notions of possibility, and offer themselves as beacons toward significant purpose. Often mentors know their protégés over an extended period of time; sometimes they serve only briefly in 'mentoring moments'; and some—authors for example—exercise influence only from afar (Daloz, C. H. Keen, J. P. Keen, Parks, 1996, pp. 44–45).

In 2003 Tim McGuire, a nationally-recognized journalist and lecturer, facilitated a workshop for Loyola University Chicago faculty and staff on the role of mentors in our lives. He suggested that all of us—but especially young adults—need mentors who will help us (1) understand the importance of personal search and journey—the need to continue to learn about ourselves and the world; (2) recognize the necessity of personal responsibility for our own lives—the need to own our successes and failures—to chart our own course and take ownership of our futures; and (3) discover and develop our special gifts as the key to finding our calling—to know that using our gifts will bring us and the world great joy. (McGuire 2003).

Identifying Your Mentors

So where exactly do you find people like this? Look at your life. They are probably already there, in some form or another. If you could use some assistance in naming them, use the following checklist to identify your mentors.

Read each question and fill in the name(s) of people who serve that function for you. You can and probably will list some names more than once.

1. Who are the people in your life who are willing to share their expertise?

_____

2. To whom do you turn when you need someone who will be completely honest?

_____

3. Who provides you with realistic assessments of yourself, others, and events?

_____

4. Who is best at reviewing situations rationally and analytically?

_____

5. To whom do you go when you need support?

_____

6. Who helps you identify and sort through your feelings and passions?

_____

7. Who always leaves you with something to think about?

_____

8. Who helps you set appropriate boundaries?

_____

9. Who is always willing to listen and serve as a sounding board?

_____

10. Who are the people that are willing to share themselves and their stories?

_____

11. To whom do you turn when you need permission to take risks?

_____

12. Who are your role models?

_____

13. Who are the people who serve as inspirations?

_____

You now have a list of possible mentors. These are the people who can help you dream, aspire, and create a vision of the world and your place in it. They can also help you successfully manage the here and now, thrash out current problems and issues, and attend to the important as well as the urgent. Marcia Baxter Magolda (see chapter 4) would consider these people good company for the journey into adulthood (Baxter Magolda 2002). If you haven't already done so, this would be a good time to thank your mentors for their support and encouragement. Let them know that they play a significant role in your life. It is likely that they will appreciate your acknowledgement and be honored to continue as a companion on your life's journey.

FINDING COMMUNITY

In the ancient Greek usage, 'politics' referred to whatever involved people in affairs that went beyond personal and family welfare. In this broad sense, politics can be one of the most enjoyable and most complex activities available to the individual, for the larger the social arena one moves in, the greater the challenges it presents . . .

It does not matter whether one starts to work with the Cub Scouts or with a group exploring the Great Books, or trying to preserve a clean environment, or supporting the local union. What counts is to set a goal, to concentrate one's psychic energy, to pay attention to the feedback, and to make certain that the challenge is appropriate to one's skill. Sooner or later the interaction will begin to hum . . . (Csikszentmihalyi 1990, pp. 190–191).

Becoming a part of the "body politic" is not always an easy thing for a young adult to accomplish once college is completed. While in school, there are always interesting things going on and participatory opportunities are endless. You can be "a part of something" and feel connected to a bigger life picture without much difficulty. After college, connection to a community competes with a full-time job and/or graduate program. As noted in chapter 3, it becomes more complex to fit community commitments into your life. Yet finding and participating in a community goes a very long way toward enhancing your self-esteem, giving you a sense of belonging and helping you recognize that your life has meaning. What is most striking about the book, *Quarterlife Crisis* (Robbins and Wilner 2001), is that so many of the young adults interviewed simply could not figure out how to feel good about their lives. They seemed to suffer from the "paralysis of analysis." In trying to clarify their own identity and their place in the world, they seemed to rely heavily upon isolation and introspection. The problem with this approach is that when your only tool is a mirror, it is almost impossible to develop a larger worldview. Thus it is not surprising that all they could see were their own doubts, their own flaws, and their own fear of failure.

Viktor Frankl, the famed Austrian psychiatrist who survived years in a Nazi concentration camp, would challenge the process these young adults have used to find satisfaction in their lives. He maintained that happiness cannot be achieved by wanting to be happy. Happiness, in fact, is the unintended consequence of working for a greater goal—something larger than oneself. This perspective is also emphasized in *Good Business* (Csiksentmihalyi, 2003). ". . . as human beings we continue to need the feeling that we belong to a community, to an entity greater than ourselves" (p. 56). *Good Business* studies leaders with "soul"—major corporate leaders who not only do "well" (are competent and run sound organizations) but also do "good" (are ethical and invested in having a positive impact on the world). He suggests that the most important trait that distinguishes these visionary leaders from other CEOs is their belief that what they do must benefit others as well as themselves. They are called to do their best, help their stakeholders as well as their stockholders, and to build a better world (Csikszentmihalyi 2003). He quotes Yvon Chouinard, the founder of Patagonia (manufacturer of outdoor gear):

We need a certain amount of stability in our lives. But it is not enough simply to know that the sun is going to rise the next morning, and that the robins will return in the spring. We also have to feel that despite chaos and entropy, there is some order and permanence in our relationships and that our lives are not wasted, and will leave some trace in the sands of time. In short, we must have the conviction that our existence serves a useful purpose and has value (Csikszentmihalyi 2003, p. 11).

Living a life that has meaning in a world as complex as our own is also the focus of *Common Fire*. The authors' beliefs are directly in line with Frankl's and Chouinard's. They too understand that young adults need connection to people and organizations that are challenging, supportive, and inspiring. "Practicing a consciousness of connection—whether with our families, colleagues, neighbors, the natural world, or people, places, and problems far away—can be the critical first step in learning to see how apparently diverse people, issues, and things are related" (Daloz, C. H. Keen, J. P. Keen, Parks 1996, pp. 215–216).

So where can you find community? It is useful to start with your passions. If they don't immediately leap to mind, ask yourself some questions? What types of people, things, issues are you deeply concerned about? What kind of news stories rivet you, upset you, make you angry? What would make you write a letter to the editor, to your town council, or to your congressional representative? If you were magically given an extra day each week to "do good," how would you use it?

There are also more concrete approaches. Ask other people to tell you about the community organizations in which they invest their time and energy. Identify the causes to which you have donated money or time in the past. List the community activities in which your family was involved when you were growing up. Call the Chamber of Commerce in your area. Ask the reference librarian to help you identify a listing of nonprofit organizations that seek volunteer assistance. If you love kids, become a big brother or sister. If you like to cook, contact your local meals-on-wheels program. If you adore animals, look to the zoo or shelters for opportunities.

Finding a community demands becoming one of the people who "are bound up with one another, sharing, despite differences, a common identity. When this transition happens well, it marks an emancipation from the literal and concrete world of child-in-the-neighborhood into the strength of a growing and more reflective person-in-community" (Daloz, C. H. Keen, J. P. Keen, Parks, 1996 p. 37). This transition is absolutely essential to finding meaningful relationships as a young adult.

JOURNAL STARTERS

1. What do you need from your family to better manage your post-college transitions?

2. What is your reaction to the following quote from *Quarterlife Crisis*? "I often say to my friends that I think there are two paths in our twenties that we are very concerned about. One is career and one is falling in love, and I think what it all has to do with is avoiding a feeling of loneliness"(p. 165).

3. Compare your best and worst team experiences. What are the key distinctions between these teams? How did you help or hinder each team?

4. Identify a person and/or organization that inspires you. How can you act upon that inspiration?

FYI

www.crossroads-center.org—The Crossroads Center has developed into a place, a community, and a resource for learning and development. Members share a passion for faith/work issues—specifically the integration of these two important parts of their lives.

www.quarterlifecrisis.com—Abby Wilner is webmaster of this site, which acts as headquarters to a network of support groups for twentysomethings.

www.transitionsbookplace.com—Transitions Learning Center (TLC) is an extension of Transitions Bookplace of Chicago. TLC shares the bookstore's philosophy to encourage and guide people on their journey of self-discovery. The Learning Center continues the tradition of Transitions' dedication to personal growth, inward exploration, and the pursuit of spirituality.

www.twentysomething.com—Twentysomething, Inc. is a consulting and research firm that focuses exclusively on young adults (15–34 year olds), tracking lifestyle needs, language, mindset, and culture.

REFERENCES

Baxter Magolda, M. (2002, Jan-Feb). Helping students make their way to adulthood. *About campus.* pp. 2–9.

Csikszenmihalyi, M. (1990). *Flow.* NY: Harper & Row.

Csikszenmihalyi, M. (2003). *Good business.* NY: Viking Penguin.

Csikszenmihalyi, M. and Schneider, B. (2000). *Becoming adult.* NY: Basic Books.

Daloz, L. P., Keen, C. H., Keen, J. P. and Parks, S. D. (1996). *Common fire.* Boston: Beacon Press.

Greenberg, J. and Baron, R. A. (2000). *Behavior in organizations* (7th ed.). Upper Saddle River, NJ: Prentice-Hall.

McGuire, T. J. (2003). *Tell the stories, not the story.* Speech presented at the EVOKE Summer Institute for Loyola University Chicago. Delavan, WI.

Robbins, A. and Wilner, A. (2001). *Quarterlife crisis.* NY: Penguin Press.

Rogers, F. (2003). *The world according to Mister Rogers: Important things to remember:* NY: Hyperion.

8

Working to Your Heart's Content

When you leave college, there are thousands of people out there with the
same degree you have; when you get a job, there will be thousands of
people doing what you want to do for a living. But you are the only
person alive who has sole custody of your life. Your particular life. Your
entire life . . . Not just the life of your mind, but the life of your heart.
Not just your bank account, but your soul.

ANNA QUINDLEN (2000)

Most of you have had various career goals over the course of your lifetimes. Cowboy, ballerina, astronaut, super hero, rock star, super
model—all may have had their place in the pantheon of your dreams
about growing up. More often than not these career daydreams are replaced
by more practical, more attainable ways of life. Still, if you look hard enough,
you may be able to find the cowboy in the options trader or the rock star in
the junior high teacher.

In this chapter, you will search for those threads that create the tapestry of
your life. What are the themes that guide your life choices? How do these
themes impact your search for your calling . . . your decisions about how
you earn a living . . . your vision of the interface between who you are and
who you wish to be in the world?

DOESN'T PICKING A MAJOR ANSWER
ALL THE IMPORTANT QUESTIONS?

As someone who will soon graduate or has recently finished college, you've gone through the "trauma" of selecting your major. So everything is settled, right? Hardly! Picture yourself in a very big building with many rooms. Each room has a window that offers you a particular view of the world. On one side of the building, there is a park with trees and an expansive lawn that leads to a beach and a great lake. The park can't really be seen from the upper floors, but the water flowing to meet the horizon is in full view. Another side of the building faces an enormous city with bustling traffic and pedestrians walking hurriedly. The upper floors on this side show off an amazing skyline. In fact, the entire world is out there, but you will pick the view that most resonates with the person you are. Your room and window determine your worldview.

Choosing a major is very much like picking your room. Your major offers a view of the world that fits with something inside of you. It also shapes and sharpens your worldview. To be sure, the rest of the world is still there, and other people have chosen other academic disciplines as the lens through which they will view the world. Each lens is correct, and each has its limitations. No window offers a 360-degree view.

Major Mythology

There are many myths surrounding the issue of why majors are selected and how important they really are to your future. For your consideration, presented here are the top five myths about college majors.

Myth #1: You should find a career that is directly related to your major or your college education has been a waste of time and money.

Truth #1: Within five years of college graduation, six out of ten grads are working in positions that relate only indirectly to their undergraduate major. What this tells us is that asking the question, "What can I do with a major in _____ (fill in the blank with your major)?" is not particularly useful. Most undergraduate majors are basic preparation for many different career paths. Your college major is only one of the many factors that should be considered when you are investigating careers.

Myth #2: Once you have selected a major, you are on a direct route to a career.

Truth #2: Deciding who you want to be in the world is never a straight line. In fact, serendipity is a major contributor to everyone's development—personal and professional. You never want to be so locked into your plans that you ignore options or refuse to accept realities.

Myth #3: Knowing is always better than not knowing.

Truth #3: While planning is essential to career development, it doesn't always lead to clear-cut, once-and-for-all decisions. There is a great deal of ambiguity inherent in any decision-making process. While it is not very comfortable, it is imperative that you allow for moments when you simply "do not know." If you try to fill in all the blanks before you have allowed yourself to explore and seek your own truth, you may grab on to some answers. However, these answers don't often hold up under the pressure of day-to-day life.

"If you can see the path laid out in front of you, step by step—it's not your path."

Joseph Campbell

Myth #4: If you do all the right things, you will move smoothly toward your career goals with no interruptions, changes, or disappointments.

Truth #4: Not! While you have control over your choices and behaviors, you cannot control the thoughts, feelings, and actions of others; nor can you always anticipate the impact of local, national, and global events on your personal and professional world. Any of these things can affect your journey positively or negatively. As the "Serenity Prayer" suggests, it takes real wisdom to recognize what you can and cannot change.

Myth #5: Your choice of major provides you with all the information needed to select a satisfying career.

Truth #5: Picking your major is just the beginning. Donald Super defined "career" as the sum total of one's life's work. There are many other things that impact your vision of your future. These are the things that we will look at next.

HEY, DOES BEING A GROWN-UP COME WITH DIRECTIONS?

Wouldn't it be wonderful if there *were* an instruction book to follow—some map to get you through young adulthood? While there is nothing simple about "crossing-over" from college student to independent adult, there are some overall guidelines that might prove useful.

Big Questions . . . Important Answers

Here is a rather intuitive approach to determining what's important to you right now. Complete the following sentences.

Passion—What drives you? What makes you smile? What do you never tire of talking about? You have no doubt heard the phrases, "do what you love and the money will follow" and "follow your passion." Creating a career based on *something that is as important to you as the air you breathe* is not only possible but also desirable.

*I am passionate about my involvement in/with*_____

_____

In a September 24, 2001 address at Loyola University Chicago, Mark Albion, author, educator, and consultant, discussed a study on passion and work. The subjects of this study, conducted from 1960 to 1980, were 1500 business school graduates who fell into two distinct groups. Group A contained the individuals who selected their first job on the basis of money, believing that they would get to their passions later in their career. 83% or 1245 of the people studied fell into Group A. The remaining 17%, or 255 subjects, elected to find work that they were passionate about regardless of money. At the conclusion of this 20-year study, 101 of the subjects were multimillionaires. Group A produced one (1) of the 101. The other 100 came from the group of individuals who chose to follow their passion (Albion 2000).

Interests—What is so interesting to you that, when you're involved in it you forget to eat, sleep, check your messages? What makes you late for work? . . . for a date? . . . for dinner?

I often loose track of time when I _____

_____

When I grow up—What was your very first calling and why did it call your name? Can that piece—that thread—still exist in your work or in your life? How would you incorporate this thread, the critical part of your first calling, into your world today?

*The first thing I remember wanting to be when I grew up was*_____

_____

Values—Everyone works for reasons beyond the obvious paycheck. What makes work satisfying for you? Your work could offer you power, affiliation, intellectual status, or the opportunity to positively impact others. Knowing what you *need from a job* is as important as having the skills necessary to do the job. Everyone hopes to lay claim to their values through their work, and the folks who do so are likely to find their work meaningful.

In order for me to love my work, it would have to meet my need(s) for _____

_____

Dreams—Do you have a dream job? What makes it perfect? Can you find those things in "real" work? What would it take to move you from the work you do now to the work you dream about? Who and what would provide support? Who and what would block your path?

In a perfect world, my job would be _____

_____

> "What can be more satisfying than to be engaged in work in which every capacity or talent one may have is needed, every lesson one may have learned is used, every value one cares about is furthered?"
>
> *John Gardner*

Lifestyle—Where would you be living? How would you be living? Who are the key people in your life? How does your job enhance your life? Is your life bigger than your work? What are the pieces of your life that contribute to your ability to respond to your calling?

In a perfect world, my life would be _____

_____

Something bigger than yourself—What are the gifts you will bequeath to the world? If people were describing you in a phrase or sentence, what do you hope they would say?

In the end, I would like people to remember me for _____

_____

You may not be able to answer all these questions immediately, however, you may be surprised by how quickly you can respond to some. It is important to write down your answers and keep them close at hand. Look at your responses and the patterns that emerge. Your particular set of values, interests, skills, talents, needs, and passions will come to the foreground. This picture of "whom you hope to be and what you hope to do in the world" will be your guide as you make your career and your life decisions. Oscar Wilde once said, "I use my talent for writing, but I save my genius for living."

Other Paths to the Truth about You

It is always helpful to employ several techniques when you are trying to answer the "Who am I?" question. This section offers a number of approaches for you to use.

Find a Guide You probably have a number of "older and wiser" people in your life. They may be relatives, friends, teachers, employers, acquaintances—anyone whom you admire and find interesting. Ask them how they negotiated the transitions of young adulthood. What did they do after college? Was their first job the right job? What did they do well? What do they wish they had done better? What is their perspective on you? Ask for their suggestions; listen to their advice. Make them a part of your network. Keep in touch with them.

They will continue to be invaluable resources as you make decisions about the path that your career and your life will take.

Use the Professionals Most colleges and universities have career centers that provide both career development and job search services to students and alumni. Begin gathering information about the services and programs of your career center by checking out their website. You can usually find information about location, office hours, a list of upcoming programs and events sponsored by the center, and links to a range of career information and job hunting websites. Many career centers also list campus and local events that have a career focus. For instance, centers typically advertise job fairs sponsored by other organizations, presentations by various professional associations, or speakers brought to campus by academic departments.

In addition to this type of information, many career center websites use interactive databases that allow students and alumni to post their resumes. Employers seeking candidates for internships as well as full-time work can access the databases to review posted resumes and/or list available positions. If you are looking for an internship, a part-time job, or a full-time position, you simply go to your career center's website and log on to their particular database program. You can review jobs and, often, you can also apply on-line from anywhere at anytime as long as you have access to a computer.

The most important connection you can make at the career center, however, is with a career counselor. Whether you are a student or a graduate, developing an ongoing relationship with a career center counselor can be helpful at any and every stage of the career decision-making and job search process. While most career counselors work with you individually, some offer the option to work in a small group setting. Many career counselors also teach workshops and/or courses for credit.

When you meet with a career counselor for the first time, he/she will typically start out by asking what your particular concerns are. From your perspective, any issue you have that relates to your thoughts about majors, careers, or calling is completely fair game. Sometimes these conversations flip a switch and an idea or direction gets considerably clearer. Sometimes these conversations generate as many questions as answers. If that's the case, you can use your time with the counselor to design strategies to gather more information about yourself and/or the world. Some counselors may use career-related inventories to help you clarify your interests and skills and show you how to relate them to occupational options. Career/life planning courses are offered in many schools and, if you are still a student, a counselor might encourage you to register for this type of class.

Sometimes people are disappointed with their initial visit to a career counselor. Secretly, they hope that a counselor will tell them what to do; that they can walk away with a decision made. It is important to understand that the purpose of career counseling is not to tell you what or whom you should be; rather, it is to guide you in your search for those answers. The process sometimes gets personal; however, careers and callings are very personal things. We encourage you to meet with a career counselor and to check out your career center's other resources. Whether you are a student or a recent graduate, take advantage of everything your school's career center has to offer.

University Mentors In chapter 7 you looked at the role that mentors can play in your adjustments to "the real world." It is often easy to overlook the obvious mentors in your life—faculty and staff advisors. These people have worked with you throughout your collegiate career and can be enormously helpful in launching the next phase of your work life. These are the people who know your skills and talents well because they have had four years to observe your efforts and guide you in cultivating your abilities. You may have consciously or unconsciously used a number of these people as role models. Now is the time to talk to them! Let them know the options that you are considering. Let them know what your concerns are. Ask for assistance. Most often, they are more than happy to continue to guide and support you.

Read a Book Your local bookstore is filled with books on career planning and job search. The topics in these books almost always fall into three main categories—self-assessment, career research, and job search techniques—but the approaches vary. Browse a bit in order to find the book that fits you best. And then, *buy it* because you will want to write in it, do the exercises, look at it again in a few years. Review the references and fyi sections at the end of this chapter for suggestions.

Surf the Web Everyone knows about the job search websites, but there are many other sites that offer career information and a host of career-related resources. Most college and university career centers have websites that not only outline their own programs but also link you to other useful sites. They are often the best place to start. Check out the list at the end of this chapter.

Act as If Experience is, perhaps, the best teacher. While you can learn a great deal by thinking, observing, and talking, there is no substitute for doing. Action can take many forms and most often the form is irrelevant. A paying job is one way to expand your experience and develop skills, but it is certainly not the only way. The wisdom of Will Rogers provides a homespun but nevertheless true insight into "acting as if . . ." He said, "Even if you're on the right track, you'll get run over if you just sit there!"

WHILE YOU'RE WAITING
FOR YOUR "REAL" JOB

Even the most dedicated job hunter can spend months finding that first professional position. These months, while difficult, can also be used to gain valuable experience to enhance your marketability.

Volunteer Every community needs volunteers and many organizations have formal volunteer programs. Consider volunteer opportunities within an organization (i.e., hospitals, schools, community service agencies, theaters) or for a professional association (many associations have "student" and/or "young professional" affiliates.) As a volunteer, you can strengthen your experience, develop your skills, and expand your personal and professional networks.

Take an Internship Internships are not only a means of developing higher levels of knowing (see chapter 4), they are also excellent opportunities to test your interests and hone your skills. In Anne Fisher's July 1, 2002 column for Fortune.com, she responded to a question about the value of internships.

> ". . . take the internship, learn all you can, make as many contacts within the company as possible, and work hard to show them what you can do. Surveys show that employers who hire interns end up offering a "real" job to 60% of them, and that's the 60% you want to be in. Even if no full time position comes through . . . you'll have gained some valuable job experience." (Fisher 2002)

Emily was a student in a career planning class. Case in Point 8.1 contains her true story, which is a testament to the value of internships.

CASE IN POINT 8.1   Emily's Internship

Emily was a recent graduate with degree in biology. Throughout her undergraduate experience, she had considered a number of medical careers but never felt completely satisfied with any of them. The source of her doubts was the fact that she also loved research and animals—especially the great apes. In fact she had considered the possibility of devoting her life to the study of their behavior.

Since this path would require a doctorate in zoology, as well as relocation, Emily decided that an internship was an important prerequisite to a commitment of this magnitude. She was selected as an intern by a top-tier zoo that was conducting behavioral research with apes. She was thrilled with the opportunity and knew it would certainly improve her chances of being accepted into a strong graduate program.

A funny thing happened to Emily on her way to her career in animal behavioral research. To her surprise, she discovered that the reality of doing this type of research bored her beyond her wildest dreams. While a bit disappointed in the unanticipated outcome of her internship, Emily felt that the experience was invaluable. She learned first-hand that theory and practice are often very different. She could cross applying to zoology programs off her "to-do" list and let go of animal research as a career choice. She was now completely free to pursue a career in health care and did so with absolutely no hesitation. Emily understood inherently that her "bad internship experience" was as useful to her in clarifying her career path as a positive experience would have been. Either way, Emily won!

Internships come in a wide range of formats. Some employers seek interns on a part-time basis and are usually willing to work around a school schedule. Other employers may require a full-time commitment for a specified period of time. While most people complete one or several internships during their undergraduate careers, post-graduation internships are often available and can be very useful.

Most colleges and universities offer academic credit for internship experience. The rules governing credit differ from school-to-school and sometimes among academic disciplines within the same university. Check with your academic advisor or career counselor *before* you obtain an internship, if you are interested in receiving academic credit for the experience.

Money is another variable in the internship equation. Some internships include a per hour wage or a stipend, however, these positions are the exception. In fact unpaid internships are the norm in many industries. You are trading your time and talent for experience and exposure. Given the short-term nature of most internship experiences, it is a fair and often a necessary trade.

Do the "Temp" Thing Temporary employment also offers career information, networking contacts, skill building, rent money, and, in some cases, benefits. Looking for a temp job in the occupation or industry that fits your career interests is always a good idea. For instance, a biology grad seeking a research career might choose to work for a lab temp agency and build direct skills and experience while making herself more employable.

Bright, new grads in service roles also have a terrific opportunity to meet and have on-going contact with seasoned professionals. These professionals are often more than willing to help out a young person who has provided them with top-notch customer service. You can use your job as a barista, a health club attendant, or a waiter as a platform to make contacts and develop relationships with individuals who can mentor you. Read Case in Point 8.2 to learn how one new grad really benefited by keeping his long-standing summer job.

AND NOW, A WORD FROM THE CAREER THEORY AUTHORITIES

Knowing and understanding yourself is an enormous job for any individual. It requires a willingness to embrace your past and present, your gifts and challenges, your sense of the divine and the mundane. The information you have gathered, analyzed, and synthesized about the person you are creates a personal template to serve as a guide when sorting through occupational information.

Most career theories provide you with a structured way to think about the points of intersection between the world of work and personality patterns. While the theories may have dramatic differences, they all exist to help you find work that is satisfying and fits with your personal template.

CASE IN POINT 8.2   Brian's Summer Job

Every summer since he was sixteen, Brian caddied at a local country club. He also had several other "typical student" jobs and interned in the marketing department of a Fortune 500 company during his junior year of college. He did all the right things during his senior year to find a job in marketing. He used his university's career center. He went to job fairs. He applied to positions he found on-line and in the paper. Unfortunately for Brian, the 2002 job market was a tight one and despite his best efforts, he found himself a graduate of a Big 10 school and unemployed.

So Brian did what he did every summer—he caddied. His parents were not pleased with his choice and wanted him to involve himself in something that was related to marketing. However, Brian needed time for a job search and the quick cash that caddying provided.

At first he felt guilty about his choice, however, something

unanticipated began to happen. As a caddie, Brian worked for many people who had known him since he was in high school. They asked him where he was in school and what his plans were. He said that he had just graduated and his plan was to find a job in marketing. Then they asked him for his resume to pass on to friends and colleagues. They gave him names and numbers of marketing professionals. They told him that he could use them as a reference. They even arranged some "face time" with executives who could assist him. He also had several interviews as a result of their connections.

None of these people knew Brian, the marketing major, but they knew and thought highly of Brian, the dedicated, bright, and pleasant caddie. That knowledge was all they needed to be willing to extend a hand to a new professional struggling in a tough market place.

Birds of a Feather Work Together—
John Holland's Theory of Vocational Choice

The research and insight of psychologist John Holland redefined prevailing views about how people choose careers. Holland recognized that individuals in the same occupation seemed to have a lot in common. His research and the subsequent research generated by his work validated the concept the individuals with similar values, interests, and skills tend to find satisfaction in similar work.

As Holland's research continued, he determined that six broad classifications could be used to categorize both individual personality and specific jobs. These themes are realistic, investigative, artistic, social, enterprising and conventional (Holland 1985).

The Realistic Theme A realistic person is interested in the world of things. This world is defined by Holland to include animals, agriculture, machinery, athletics, nature, and jobs that have an element of risk to them. It is a world inhabited by practical people who like "hands-on" work, enjoy interacting with the environment, and prefer a physical component to their work and play. Firefighters, forest rangers, mechanics, police officers, animal trainers, landscape architects, and carpenters are a sample of careers that are dominantly realistic.

The Investigative Theme Investigative people are also interested in the world of things but in a theoretical or conceptual way. The investigators like to think about, observe, and research things. They enjoy generating ideas and conducting research that demonstrates whether those ideas hold water, however, they are not concerned if their ideas and theories have no practical application in the present. Biologist, physicist, chemist, mathematician, physician, psychologist, sociologist, systems analyst are among the job titles in the investigative theme.

The Artistic Theme Artistic people also like the world of ideas but these folks are interested in using their creativity to give their ideas form. Their ideas can take the form of a dance, a symphony, a play, a novel, a painting, a logo, a legal brief, a floral arrangement, a gourmet dinner, a news broadcast, etc. It is important to keep in mind that "creativity," as Holland defines it, is not the sole purview of the fine arts. It is a much broader concept that focuses on an individual's unique perspective about the world. Many artistic people have never put paint to a canvas or played the cello. They apply their creativity to activities like brainstorming or problem solving.

The Social Theme Individuals who are social are also creative and choose to use their creativity in the service of other people. The social theme houses many of the helping professions, including teaching, ministry, counseling, social work, nursing, and coaching. You may notice that occupations like nursing or counseling fall into the social category, but physician and psychologist are investigative careers. It can be helpful to think of this as a distinction between practice and theory. Social people are interested in providing direct service to others. They want to be actively involved with the people they are assisting and with the helping process. Investigators, on the other hand, are more interested in diagnosis and creating a treatment plan. They leave the application of the treatment to the social folks. For instance, a doctor reads the chart, assesses symptoms, makes a medical diagnosis, and determines a course of treatment; it is left to a nurse to administer medication, and explain the treatment plan and necessary follow-up procedures to the patient.

The Enterprising Theme Enterprising people are also interested in working with others. Their focus, however, is leading, influencing, directing, or persuading others, and they use data or information to do it. People whose job titles suggest that they are in charge (e.g., supervisor, administrator, director, manager, vice president, CEO, etc.) fall into the enterprising theme. Broad occupational areas that are enterprising include law and politics, sales and marketing, merchandising, small business ownership, etc.

One of Holland's more confusing findings is about law and lawyers. Law is an enterprising field and "judge" is an enterprising career—the focus of both the field and the career is on influencing and directing. However, "attorney" falls into the artistic category, because an attorney relies on his/her creativity or unique perspective on the law to give form to an argument in court or a legal brief.

The Conventional Theme The last Holland theme is conventional. People who gravitate toward conventional careers are primarily interested in data. Their jobs usually focus on taking large amounts of raw information and putting it into a useable framework. Accountants, credit analysts, bankers, travel agents, meeting planners, and administrators of all kinds are primarily conventional.

The theory goes on to suggest that this classification system can be used to match people to jobs that would provide them with satisfying work. Holland maintains that every individual can identify with two or three of the six themes. There is usually one theme that is dominant. Your combination of themes is called your Holland Code. Once you know your Holland Code you can reference a list of careers that matches your code. For instance, if you are investigative/realistic (IR) you might be interested in veterinary medicine, engineering, or botany. Someone with an investigative/artistic code might enjoy architecture or consider becoming a plastic surgeon. An enterprising/ social/conventional (ESC) person might make a good nonprofit administrator, public health nurse/manager, or funeral home director.

If you have ever taken the Self-Directed Search (SDS) or the Strong Interest Inventory (SII), you have, in fact, worked with John Holland's theory of vocational choice. These instruments can be particularly helpful if you have no clear concept of careers. When completed, these inventories provide you with a list of occupational possibilities. As you investigate the careers on your list that are interesting to you, you can expand your understanding of yourself and your fit in the world.

These inventories are also helpful if you find yourself at the other end of the spectrum—one of those folks who wants to do everything. Because the results of these assessment instruments are rank-ordered, they suggest which occupations might provide a "best fit." Either way, the SII and the SDS provide you with a place to start.

Expect the Unexpected—Good Advice
from John Krumboltz

Social learning theory of career decision making, the late-70s brainchild of John Krumboltz, examines why people choose to enter or change educational programs or occupations at various points in their lives. In order to answer these questions, this theory suggests that the career decision-making process considers four major factors: genetic endowment and special abilities; environmental conditions and events; learning experiences; and task approach skills. In combination, these factors influence what individuals come to believe about themselves and the world. These beliefs color one's sense of efficacy regarding the acquisition of new skills and ultimately what one is capable of accomplishing. In 1991 Krumboltz's Career Beliefs Inventory became available as a career decision-making tool. This instrument assesses an individual's belief system and identifies obstacles blocking his or her ability to act on career decisions.

In the last decade, Krumboltz, with Kathleen Mitchell and Al Levin, have recognized the significant role that chance plays in every person's career. This theory is called "planned happenstance." It proposes that unplanned events, which are not only inevitable but also desirable, are opportunities for learning. It goes on to suggest that anyone's career development would be best served if they are willing and able to be curious, persistent, flexible, optimistic, and take action in the face of uncertain outcomes. (Mitchell, Levin, and Krumboltz 1999, p. 118)

> "From one point of view, it could be said that unplanned events affect 100% of career choices. No one chooses his or her own parents, place and date of birth, and first language or initial educational experiences, yet these events inevitably affect subsequent career paths . . . Prior research indicates that the majority of those studies attributed major responsibility to unplanned events, for example, 57% of workers (in general); 72% of college graduates." (Mitchell, Levin, and Krumboltz 1999, p. 122)

The conclusions drawn by Krumboltz tell us that career decision making is a "complex and fascinating process that involves both personal and work-related issues, knowledge and wisdom about the realities and possibilities of life . . ." (Mitchell, Levin, and Krumboltz 1999, p. 123). Carmen's story in Case in Point 8.3 is a real life example of the ways in which the unplanned affects career opportunities.

Work Should Be Fun—A Gift from Edward Bordin

Edward Bordin was a counseling psychologist who believed that our approach to career development was much too serious. While he made a number of significant contributions to the field, perhaps the two most important were: (1) to warn people that the "test 'em and tell 'em" approach to career decision making (allowing the results of a career inventory to determine the "right" occupation for an individual) was inadequate at best; and, (2) to develop the idea that a person's work should be an avenue for expressing his or her playfulness.

Bordin took a psychodynamic approach to career choice in that he was one of the first theorists to recognize the impact of an individual's history on career development. As Bordin saw it, one's career identity was primarily a function of parental influence, family systems and dynamics, and the emerging self-concept of the child. Career assessment instruments, while helpful, do not focus on these concepts.

His legacy, however, is the concept of the fusion of work and play. Estela Rivero, now a university administrator, was one of Bordin's graduate students. Because he was her dissertation co-chair, she discussed her anxiety about her upcoming dissertation defense with him. He said that she was probably concerned that spending several hours face-to-face with a panel of experts answering questions about her research wouldn't be any fun. He assured her that they would have a lively discussion that would, indeed, be enjoyable. Rivero said, "Thus, my anxiety dissipated, the orals were a rite of passage in the most positive sense—and I learned about the key role of playfulness in work." (Goodyear, Roffey, and Jack 1994, p. 563)

CASE IN POINT 8.3 The Unexpected Dividends of Carmen's Creativity

Carmen was graduating with a sociology degree during a time of record unemployment. She knew she "wanted to work with people"—knowledge that didn't do much to distinguish her from all of the other about-to-be college grads looking for work.

In her last semester, she was inspired by the instructional style of an American history professor who was new to the university. He gave his students a great deal to think about and enormous room to use their creativity in producing the final project for the course. Carmen made many of her own clothes and chose to make a dress for her final history project. Her task was to create a style and select material that related in some way to the content of the class. She had no idea what his response to her project would be, but it was her last semester and she was willing to take the chance.

She came to the meeting for her final project in the dress she had made. She explained why she

had chosen that particular medium and how the dress related to the course. Carmen got an "A" on the project, but she also got something she had not planned on. When they were finished discussing her dress, her professor asked what her plans were after graduation. Carmen replied that she needed a job and hoped to "work with people." He asked a few more questions, and Carmen mentioned that one area of interest for her was settlement house work.

When she said this, she had no idea that he sat on the metropolitan board for settlement houses. Her professor gave her the name of an executive director of a settlement house in the area and encouraged her to use his name as a reference. He also contacted the executive director on her behalf. Carmen called, interviewed, and was offered a position. She began her job two weeks after graduation—a job that emerged because she took a professor up on his offer to be creative and impressed him by doing so.

Even before Csikszentmihalyi's groundbreaking research on the psychology of optimal experience (see chapter 9 for information on "flow"), Edward Bordin was giving us permission and encouragement to combine the imperative of earning a living with the imperative of fun, play, and self-expression.

CONNECTING TO YOUR CALLING

"Images of the self that encourage high aspiration and excellence . . . enable the young adult to see beyond self and world as they presently are and to discern a vision of the potential of life: *the world as it ought to be and the self as it might become.*"

Sharon Daloz Parks (2000)

The first place to look for answers to life's puzzles, conflicts, and demands is in the mirror. Your history, your sense of self, your goals, needs, values, skills, and interests will be the determining factors in the choices you make and the paths you choose. This chapter has given you a number of techniques you can use to achieve some insight and clarity as you strive to answer the "who am I" question, recognizing that you are the only one with access to the information. Since the process of shaping your life and your work never ceases, you will need to answer this question again and again throughout your life.

Knowing who you are is only one-half of the equation. The other 50 percent requires recognizing what theologian, Frederick Buechner, referred to as "the world's deep hunger" (1993). If you understand the ways in which the person you are and the needs of the larger world intersect, you have some idea about your calling. The question then broadens from "what can I do that will make me happy?" to "what can I do that will give me purpose?" Erica, an undergraduate student, puts it this way, "I think a calling is something that is with you forever in some ways even if you are not necessarily practicing it. I think it will be something that I cannot see myself not doing or being without in my life." Greg, a junior, suggests, ". . . that the 'Spirit' at work in the world through us is, in a sense, our calling. The Spirit is a combination of many 'small steps and minor achievements'." Leslie, also a junior, offers, "I know that if I say 'yes' to whatever my calling could be I will be happy and it will give my life a sense of meaning . . . if I say 'no,' I think I will always notice that there is something missing in my life."

Each of these students is wrestling with his or her private concept of calling. They are watching for signs and hoping that, eventually, things will gel for them. They don't have the answers, and might not for a while, but they are open to the possibilities, even though staying open is overwhelming and more than a little scary at times. Michael, a junior, sums up his anxiety about the process, ". . . I have all the resources I need, I have all the help anyone could ask (for) . . . the only person holding me back is me . . . sometimes I feel I will never know what's there for me . . . there are just so many things I can do . . . but will I make it? Will I like it? What is it that is meant for me?"

Listening for and decoding your calling is a process, not a single "ah-ha" moment or one-time experience. It is hard work and it has some risks. But it is worth the trouble.

CONSTRUCTING YOUR JOB SEARCH

Deciding what you want to do is certainly the central task of shaping a satisfying career. After you have put time and energy into identifying what your work will be, your next step is finding a place to do that work. Because this step—the job search—is the most obvious and most concrete component of career planning, it is often viewed as the entry point rather than the last phase of the career development process. It may be tempting to skip the difficult tasks of defining yourself in terms of your values, skills, interests, and vision, and of synthesizing these personal elements with the needs of the world. However, it is not in your best interests! It you have not clarified and taken ownership of a career direction, your job search becomes a very real burden. You will end up working twice as hard to get half as far.

Nebulous resumes written without a target audience in mind are ineffective marketing tools. Pat interview answers that focus on what you hope the interviewer wants to hear reveal that you have nothing useful or insightful to say. The moral of the story is that the thought and energy you put into assessing yourself and your world has huge dividends when it is time for you to conduct a job search.

The essential tools of an effective job search are a strong, targeted resume; directed and personalized cover and thank you letters; and researched and thoughtful answers to interview questions. Your goal is to acquire these tools and get comfortable using them.

People on Paper: The Art of Resume Writing

A truly effective resume achieves two objectives: (1) it presents a concise summary of your skills and accomplishments; and, (2) it clearly establishes a relationship between your experience and your career objective. The challenge of resume writing is that you must be both creative and able to work in a clearly prescribed structure. Although there are some specific rules to resume writing, your goal is to develop a unique piece, outstanding for its personalized content and its visual appeal. Producing an exceptional resume is exceptionally hard work, but worth the struggle. The employer interest that is generated by a top-notch resume will be the reward for your effort.

Content Clues Write your own resume. Your resume should be authentic and accurately reflect your goals and achievements. You are the best person to accomplish this task. Writing your resume also forces you to organize, analyze, and articulate your experience—a process that enhances your interview technique.

Use the thesaurus. Select specific action verbs that convey your experience, results, etc., as clearly as possible. Choose nouns, adjectives, and adverbs with the same outcome in mind. Selectively use professional jargon or industry "buzzwords." Do not repeat the same verbs or nouns throughout your resume. Do not use pronouns.

Brief is better. Use phrases instead of sentences. Avoid paragraphs. Make your point and move on.

Anatomy of a Resume Resumes are made up of component parts, and not every section will be applicable to you. The heading and objective are the first two sections of a resume; other sections can be listed in the order that best markets you.

The *Heading* consists of your full name, street address, city, state, zip code, phone number(s), and e-mail address. Your *Career Objective* requires you to define your career goals. Your objective is the thesis statement of your resume, creating a frame of reference for the reader. The format and content of your resume must be created to reflect this reference point.

The *Education* section is a listing of degrees achieved, schools attended, and areas of study pursued, with the most recent degree appearing first. *Certifications and Licenses* can be a subsection of Education. You may also list *Coursework* that supports your career objective (maximum of six classes). Thesis work, academic honors, and grade point average are typically recorded in this section as well. However, if you have numerous *Honors and Awards,* you may want to list them in a separate section. Like honors, *Co-curricular Activities* may be a subsection of education or may appear separately. Co-curricular involvement, wherever it is listed, should include the organizations in which you are/were an active participant, offices held, and the outcomes of your efforts.

The *Experience* section can be a mixture of paid and unpaid work, listed in reverse chronological order. Each experience includes your position title, your dates of service (year-to-year is sufficient), and the organization's name, city, and state. The skills you demonstrated as well as the results of your work are highlighted. Whenever possible, it is useful to quantify and/or qualify the outcomes of your efforts. If it markets you more effectively, you can design a section called *Professional Skills* or *Related Professional Experience* to focus the reader on specific experiences that relate directly to your career objective. In this way you can select accomplishments from education, employment, co-curricular involvement, community activities, etc., and list them together in a targeted section.

Community Involvement allows you to detail the results of your volunteer work in terms of accomplishments and skills. A *Special Skills* section is particularly important if you are proficient in other languages, have an array of computer skills, or have other skills that directly connect to your career objective. *Professional Memberships* include the full name of the organization and dates of membership. *Military Service* notes the branch of service, dates of service, and rank upon discharge.

References available upon request. This line can appear at the bottom of your resume if there is space. You may say, "References and writing samples . . ." or "References and portfolio . . ." if you are in a field that requires these additional items. Never list the names of your references on your resume.

Resumes Need Style The style or format you choose for your resume is essential to its impact. The style you select should bring your most important accomplishments and experience to the top of your resume and focus the reader on those skills, experiences, or achievements that connect most clearly with your career goals. The two most common resume styles are *chronological* and *targeted.*

A *chronological resume* (see Table 8.1) is the most widely used format and the one most familiar to employers. This resume style is arranged in reverse chronological order, with the most recent experience listed first in each section. This format focuses on the positions held and emphasizes the progression of your work experience. If the experience you have is career-related and reflects the skills you wish to use in your next job, this style will serve you well. If there is not a direct correlation between your previous experience and your future goals, however, this format will not focus the reader on your transferable skills and potential.

Table 8.1 Chronological Resume

JOE COLLEGE
678 Main Street
Chicago, Illinois 12345
312-555-5678
jcollege@state.edu

Objective: To educate high school students in mathematics

Education: State University   Forest, Illinois
Bachelor of Science in Mathematics Education   May 2004
Certification: Illinois Type 09; Middle School Endorsement

Experience:

Summers High School   Summers, Illinois
Student Teacher, Mathematics Department   Spring 2004

- Taught three Honors Geometry classes, one Consumer Mathematics class, and an Algebra I class
- Coached selected students for Upstate 8 Math Competition

University High School   Forest, Illinois
Volunteer Instructor and Tutor   2003–2004

- Taught Algebra II to sophomore students
- Instructed juniors and seniors in Pre-calculus

Community East High School   Poplar, Illinois
Volunteer Instructor and Tutor   2002–2003

- Taught Advanced Analytic Algebra to sophomores and juniors

Niles Academy   Chicago, Illinois
Sports Camp Director   Summer 2003

- Developed a physical education summer camp program for pre-k through eighth grade students
- Directed all games and outdoor activities

Chicago Park District   Chicago, Illinois
Referee and Umpire   Seasonal 1996–2002

- Refereed for park district basketball games for children, grades 3–8
- Umpired for park district baseball games for children, grades 1–8

Computer Skills:

Microsoft Office, Geometer's Sketchpad, Fathom, Minitab

Co-curricular Activities:

Men's Softball, Men's Basketball, Men's Flag Football, Volleyball

---

A *targeted resume* (see Table 8.2) highlights the skills and experience that best correlate with the requirements of your career goal rather than your work history. It allows you to group your most important qualifications under the skill or experience headings that link directly to your career objective and place these sections toward the top of your resume. This is the format of

Table 8.2 Targeted Resume

SARAH SENIOR
321 State Street, Albany, New York 54321
123-555-1234 (cell) 123-555-4321 (home)
sarahs04@hometown.edu

Objective: A marketing position in a sports-related organization

Education: New England College, Whitecap, MA
BBA, May 2004   Major: Marketing   Minor: Sports Management
Cumulative G.P.A.: 3.72/4.0

Semester at Sea, SS Enterprise, University of Iceland, Fall 2003

Related Professional Experience:

The Rochester Ramblers Baseball Club, Buffalo, NY
Marketing Intern, Spring 2003
- Assisted in the creation and implementation of a marketing campaign that increased game attendance by 15%
- Provided administrative support to sales representatives
- Prepared information and rates packages for potential advertisers

Alumni Sports Complex, Whitecap, MA
Certified Personal Trainer, 2000–2002
- Constructed individualized fitness programs for students, faculty, and staff, including aerobics, weight training, kickboxing, and sports conditioning

The New England Wave, Whitecap, MA
Sports Editor, 2001–2002, **Sports Writer,** 2000–2001
- Covered all collegiate soccer and basketball games
- Coordinated the work of four sports writers

Skills: Exceptional writing and presentational skills; ability to work effectively in highly stressful situations and environments; strong team member

Employment:

Happy Valley Hotel, Albany, NY
Banquet Wait Staff, Seasonal 1998-present
- Promoted from waitress to supervisor to Banquet Captain
- Organize, train, and schedule a banquet staff of 20–25
- Launched and oversaw a successful promotion of banquet facilities that increased clientele by 25% in one year.

References and portfolio available upon request

---

choice if you have little or no direct experience in your chosen field. Writing a targeted resume is a greater challenge because it requires you to evaluate your past experiences in terms of the skills you acquired and demonstrate the connection between those skills and your future employment.

Layout: The Design is Worth a Thousand Words Before employers read the first word of your resume, the layout will predispose them toward a positive or a negative evaluation of your candidacy. Therefore, you need to pay particular attention to the design and production details of your resume.

A resume should never run more than two pages; one page is generally best, especially for new graduates with typical college-level experience. Your resume should allow the reader to easily scan its contents. Use blank space, font size, and indent or tab features to create an outline effect. Margins should be at least one inch on all sides and the text should appear balanced on the page. Avoid using resume templates found in some software packages because they severely limit your formatting choices.

Proofread your final draft and then ask at least two other people to proofread it. Look for improper grammar, inconsistency in language or layout, spelling or punctuation errors, poor construction of the content, typo's etc. Do not rely solely on spellcheck!

Use a high quality printer. Select good bond paper—white is preferable although very light beige or gray are acceptable. Start out with 50 copies and purchase matching paper and envelopes for all your job search correspondence.

Acing the Interview

The interview process is a two-way street. An employer uses an interview to learn whether your professional and personal attributes will be a good fit with the position and the organization. You use the process to discern whether the goals of the organization and the responsibilities of the job match your career direction, values, and skill set.

The Importance of Preparation Preparation is the key to insuring that an interview nets positive results for you and an employer. The first order of business is research, research, research. Find out as much as you can about the job for which you are interviewing. Investigate the organization and the industry. Be ready to discuss current issues and trends as well as to ask questions. Next review your responses to potential interview questions. Your answers should offer a brief, results-oriented view of your experience and skills. Study your resume in light of the position and the company. Anticipate questions and issues that might arise. Then cultivate some interview chemistry! Using the questions from Table 8.3, participate in a mock interview. Ask for feedback from friends or a career counselor. Equip yourself to calmly and pleasantly meet, greet, and communicate with the interviewer. Finally choose an interview outfit that is comfortable and professional.

And Now, the Moment You've Been Waiting For A door opens. You stand up, take a deep breath, smile, extend your hand, and introduce yourself. The interview has begun. In the few moments it took to shake hands and say hello, the interviewer has already formed some impressions about you. Your

Table 8.3 Questions to Ask and Answer

Commonly Asked Interview Questions

- Tell me about yourself. (Focus on your accomplishments as they relate to the job.)
- Why do you want to work here? (Use your research about the organization/position to reply.)
- What are your strengths? Weaknesses? (Relate them to performing the job.)
- What are your goals? (Connect this job to your career plan and/or calling.)
- Describe your most significant professional accomplishment. Your biggest challenge. (Relate these experiences to attributes you bring to this position.)
- What job did you like best? Least? (This is not the time to be hypercritical of former employers or supervisors.)
- What is your work style? What type of supervision do you prefer?
- Does your GPA accurately reflect your abilities?

Questions You Might Ask

- Request clarification about particular aspects of the job; e.g., typical day/week, reporting relationships, learning opportunities, organizational structure, etc.
- How would you describe the company's mission and management philosophy?
- How are people evaluated in the organization?
- Is there a typical career path in this area of the organization?
- What are the essential factors for success in this position?
- What are the challenges of this position?
- Where are you in the search process? What are the next steps?

promptness, appearance, verbal, and nonverbal communication skills have already been noted.

You may be involved in one interview with one person or a series of interviews with a variety of people. If you are being interviewed by a number of people, the interviews may all take place on the same day or you may be asked to come back. Since you cannot know who has seen your resume or if they still have a copy, always bring extra resumes to every interview.

Once you are sitting in the employer's office, there will probably be a bit of small talk in order to get acquainted. Take a moment to comment on an item in the office that intrigues you or suggests that you may have similar interests. The employer's goal is to gather both general and specific information about you. Be ready to expand on items in your resume and/or on your professional goals. In discussing your career objective, you can insert information you have obtained about the industry, organization, and/or the position. Comments on your background should focus on results rather than tasks. The interviewer is seeking a direct correlation between the company's needs and goals and your skills and experience. Share behavioral examples that clearly demonstrate that you possess the skills and background necessary to do the job.

Typically the interviewer will give you an opportunity to ask as well as answer questions. Use Table 8.3 to help you generate possible questions. This is also an opportunity to clarify points brought up during the interview.

As the interview comes to a close, find an opportunity to reiterate your strengths, particularly as they meet the employer's needs. Ask about follow-up procedures and leave with a business card, a handshake, and an expression of gratitude for the interviewer's time and interest.

Tips for Top-Notch Correspondence

Cover letters and thank you notes are important components of the job search. General rules to follow are:

- Use high quality stationery and envelopes that match your resume.
- Your personal heading (name, address, etc.) should match the style and format on your resume.
- Be brief (never more that one page) and error-free.
- Use a business format for all job search correspondence. Address each letter to a specific person. Ensure that all names are spelled correctly and business titles are exact.
- Remember to sign each original and keep copies of all correspondence.

Cover Letters A cover letter always accompanies a resume that is sent in response to a specific opening. Every cover letter is an original, prepared to clearly demonstrate the match between your qualifications and the employer's needs. The opening paragraph indicates your interest in the position. The body of the letter creates the connection between your skills and the position requirements. In this section, focus on the particular benefits an employer will reap if you are hired. Your final paragraph summarizes your qualifications and suggests a plan of action for further communication.

Thank You Notes Send a thank you note to anyone who has helped you in any phase of your job search. After an interview, it is particularly important to communicate appreciation and interest, and to reiterate your qualifications in relation to the field or position. Do not miss the opportunity to express your gratitude and cultivate good will.

ENVISIONING YOUR LIFE

Day-to-day living can sometimes have a hypnotizing effect. It's easy to get caught up in the "right now" and forget about the bigger picture of your life. Having a "vision *of* yourself" and a "vision *for* yourself" helps move you through the unsure and the unsafe, the all-too-comfortable plateaus and the "it's not what I really want but it will do" ruts.

In Paulo Coelho's book, *The Alchemist,* he chronicles the journey of a young shepherd who is seeking his Personal Legend. During the most difficult part of his journey, the boy has a conversation with the alchemist.

"Well, then, why should I listen to my heart?"

"Because you will never again be able to keep it quiet. Even if you pretend not to have heard what it tells you, it will always be there inside you, repeating to you what you're thinking about life and about the world. . . . you will never be able to escape from your heart. So it's better to listen to what it has to say." (Coelho 1998, p. 130–131)

JOURNAL STARTERS

1. What questions, about yourself and about the world, would you like your education to answer?

2. How have chance events affected your life? Your career decision making?

3. It's your world. What rules would you rewrite? Why?

4. What is the first career daydream you ever had? What was attractive to you about that job or role at the time? Are the things that drew you to that career present in your current career aspirations?

FYI

www.anticareer.com—Rick Jarow, author of *Creating the Work You Love*

http://career.missouri.edu/article.php?sid=146—"The Career Interests Game"

www.gregglevoy.com—Gregg Levoy, author of *Callings*

www.iccweb.com—Internet Career Connection—full service career information site

www.jobhuntersbible.com—Richard Bolles, author of *What Color Is Your Parachute?*

www.pathfinders.org—Pathfinders—"how to choose an extraordinary career path and what it takes to get there"

www.review.com—The Princeton Review—information on graduate and professional schools

www.wetfeet.com—source for occupational and industry information

REFERENCES

Albion, M. (2000). *Making a life, making a living: Reclaiming your purpose and passion in business and life.* NY: Warner Books.

Buechner, F. (1993). *Wishful thinking.* SanFrancisco, CA: HarperSanFrancisco.

Coelho, P. (1998). *The alchemist.* NY: Harper Perennial.

Fisher, A. (2002, July 1). "Taking an internship or hold out for a paying job?" www.Fortune.com.

Goodyear, R. K., Roffey A., and Jack, L. E. (1994, July/August). "Edward Bordin: Fusing work and play," *Journal of counseling & development,* Vol. 72: 563–613.

Holland, J. L. (1985). *Making vocational choices: A theory of vocational personalities and work environments*. Upper Saddle, NJ: Prentice-Hall.

Mitchell, K. E., Levin, A. S., and Krumboltz, J. D. (1999, Spring). "Planned happenstance: Constructing unexpected career opportunities," *Journal of counseling & development,* Vol. 77: 115–124.

Parks, S. D. (2000). *Big questions, worthy dreams*. SanFrancisco, CA: Jossey-Bass.

Quindlen, A. (2000). *A short guide to a happy life*. NY: Random House.

9

Looking Back
and Moving Forward

Sometimes I feel that my life is a series of trapeze swings . . . Most
of the time, I spend my life hanging on for dear life to my trapeze-bar-of-the-
moment. It carries me along at a certain steady rate of swing and I have the
feeling that I'm in control of my life . . . But once in a while . . . I see
another trapeze bar swinging toward me. It's my next step, my growth, my
aliveness going to get me . . . I know that I must totally release my grasp on
my old bar, and for some moment in time I must hurtle across space before
I can grab onto the new bar. Each time I am filled with terror . . . but I do it
anyway . . . And so for an eternity that can last a microsecond or a thousand
lifetimes, I soar across the dark void of "the past is gone, the future is not yet
here." It's called transition. I have come to believe that it is the only place that
real change occurs . . . Yes, with all the pain and fear and feelings of
being out-of-control that can . . . accompany transitions, they are still
the most alive, most growth-filled, passionate, expansive moments in our lives.

DANAAN PARRY

Given the writer Danaan Parry's point of view on transition, answer
the following question. In order to successfully negotiate the leap
through space young adults face as they take their places in careers and
communities, it is best to:

a. Look before you leap.

b. Leap and the net will appear.

c. Both a and b.

The answer is c. Both a and b. How is this paradox possible? Read on . . .

This book begins by defining "transition" as a passage from one form or condition to another. Its goal is to help you "look before you leap" (answer "a.") to the next trapeze bar. If you are reading this while still in college, this book gives you a "heads up" on the similarities and differences between success in college and success in life. If you have graduated, it is responding to concerns and issues you are currently facing. The writing of this book was driven by the comments from countless new grads that echoed sentiments expressed in Robbins and Wilner's *Quarterlife Crisis* (see chapter 7) about their decisions. It is exciting to have what often feels like limitless power to choose your life course, however, by virtue of making some choices, you eliminate others and must cope with the lingering doubts that emanate from the fact that few choices are risk-free.

> Recent graduates often agonize over their decisions; they can spend
> months trying to figure out the proper choice—or procrastinating so they
> don't have to make one in the first place. The problem is twofold. First,
> young adults often believe that the decisions they make now could
> possibly alter the course of their lives. So they feel that there is a lot riding
> on the choices they make. This pressure to make the right decisions can
> make twentysomethings feel that they need to weigh every side of an
> option before choosing one. The other reason for these smaller-scale
> doubts is that recent graduates are supposed to make important decisions
> when they hardly have any prior experience on which to base their
> reasoning. If I haven't done this before, a twentysomething reasons, then
> how do I know I am doing it right?" (Robbins and Wilner 2001, p. 123)

The goal of this book is to provide information and advice that enables you, in spite of your fears of the unknown, to leap to the next trapeze bar, confident in the belief that you can handle the challenges ahead (answer "b." above). Given the spectrum of changes you face, it is critical to understand how college has prepared you—although not fully—for the next phase of your life. It is important to recognize the tools you have already acquired and the ones you still need to attain. These key concepts are presented below, chapter by chapter, in the form of a DO-List. It is called the "A" List of ideas and advice for your *Awareness and Action*.

THE "A" LIST OF AWARENESS AND ACTION

Chapter 1 Transitions, Expectations, and the Journey Ahead

- Begin the ending phase of your transition by critically evaluating and disengaging old beliefs, e.g., strategies that helped you succeed during college will automatically help you succeed after college.

- As you complete your course requirements, pursue the activities and confront the issues that were discussed throughout this book.

- Be aware that between the ending phase and your new beginning (e.g., job, further education) is a neutral zone or limbo where old ideas and habits have not been firmly replaced by the attitudes and behaviors required for success in your new environment.

Chapter 2 From College to Corporate Culture: You're a Freshman Again

- Although your academic knowledge and skills should be important, the processes for succeeding in college and in your new work will probably differ. Review Table 2.1 Graduates' Perceived Differences between College and the Workplace.

- Get a job or an internship. Be aware that even mundane work provides an opportunity to critically examine your attitudes and preferences regarding work, develop a healthy work ethic, and gain much needed experience.

- There are four types of new employee learning tasks that you must master to succeed. Those in the all-important individual domain include the attitudes, expectations, and breaking-in-skills you carry to your first job. Prepare for individual domain tasks during college: resist the passive conditioning influences of formal education (see Table 2.1); enroll in courses that focus on workplace dimensions (management, small group skills, organizational behavior, leadership); work with a career counselor to plan your future; actively participate in organizations that emphasize teamwork; get solid work experience.

- Tasks in the people domain test your abilities to manage impressions and form healthy relationships with co-workers and supervisors. Organization domain tasks require savvy and successful adaptation to the organization's culture and roles. Work tasks are those that test and develop your knowledge and competencies in a particular area (Holton).

Chapter 3 Coming of Age: Young Adult Development

- Your transition from college to work and life is accompanied by your passage to young adulthood. Central to that passage is your ability to question and commit to a vocation and a set of values. Your goal, of course, is identity achievement (Marcia). Developing competence, control of emotions, interdependence, and mature relationships also contribute to establishing identity, purpose, and integrity (Chickering and Reisser).

- As a young adult, you construct meaning from the world by searching for the answers to life's big questions, listening to your own voice, and taking ownership of your decisions. You may become "shipwrecked" along the way, but these developmental crises are essential to personal growth. Eventually you experience the "gladness" that comes from living through a difficult experience and learning because of it (Parks).

- The journey to young adulthood is facilitated when you actively involve yourself in community; find mentors who will listen and guide you; challenge yourself to learn from "otherness" by meeting people who are not like you and visiting places unlike home; and, dream big, believing in something greater than yourself (Parks).

Chapter 4 Cognitive Development During and After College: What You Should Know About Knowing

- Be aware that the assumptions we make about our world proceed through four stages of cognitive development that include absolute, transitional, independent, and contextual knowing. Progress to higher stages is characterized by a decreasing reliance on authority for answers and increasing acceptance of uncertainty as the norm.

- Baxter Magolda's longitudinal study reveals rapid increases in independent and contextual knowing *after* students leave college and enter the workforce or graduate/professional programs. Graduates are expected to work independently, learn from and collaborate with others, benefit from direct experience, deal with uncertainty, and make subjective decisions in positions of authority.

- To facilitate your cognitive growth, enroll in student-centered courses that require group projects, participation, exams that focus on higher levels of thinking, writing, and other forms of active learning.

- In addition, you are strongly encouraged to participate in study abroad programs, internships, service learning programs, and extracurricular activities that promote teamwork, collaboration, and leadership—excellent ways to enhance independent and contextual knowing.

Chapter 5 Intelligence Revisited: What It Really Means to Be Smart

- Question the belief that intelligence is reflected primarily in IQ, test scores, or GPAs; these measures are relevant but only partial indices of what it really means to be smart in the real world.

- Successful intelligence refers to your ability to succeed, following personal standards established for your sociocultural context, and accounting for your strengths and weaknesses. Successful intelligence includes a balance of analytical, creative, and practical (implicit knowing) abilities that are used to shape, select, or adapt to environments (Sternberg).

- Emotional intelligence is the ability to accurately perceive, understand, and manage emotions. Specific abilities include self-regard, awareness, assertiveness, stress tolerance, impulse control, reality testing, flexibility, problem solving, empathy, and interpersonal skills. EI is becoming an important factor in personnel recruitment, training, communication, leadership, and team development (Ciarrochi, Forgas, and Mayer).

- Evers, Rush, and Berdrow's 18 skills (deemed important by graduates and their managers) form the four bases of competence: communicating, managing self, managing people and tasks, and mobilization and change. Become involved in those academic and co-curricular opportunities that develop or strengthen these skills.

- Create a portfolio containing evidence such as papers, projects, awards, performance evaluations, and goal statements that attest to your skill development in these and other competencies.

Chapter 6 Motivation and Learning: Principles That Work When You Do

- Try to substitute intrinsic motivation (motivational energy that arises from within you) for extrinsic rewards and outside pressures in your activities because intrinsic motives energize and sustain you for the challenges ahead.

- Establish personal and professional goals that are specific, realistic, and provide feedback. Goals can arouse and direct your energies, and they provide standards for comparing your actual with your desired outcomes (Locke and Latham).

- Be aware that your motivation is also influenced by comparisons you make between your performance and that of others, and that inequities are a reality of life (Adams). Work for equity but remain goal-oriented and intrinsically motivated.

- Motivation is influenced by the expectations we hold that: (a) our effort should lead to performance (expectancy); (b) our performance should be rewarded appropriately (instrumentality); and (c) the rewards differ in their value to us (valence) (Vroom).

- You are learning important strategies for critical thinking and problem solving, but be aware that numerous behaviors are shaped (conditioned) by intrinsic and extrinsic rewards and the tendency to model the activities of others. In addition, you develop preferences for dealing with situations characterized as learning orientations: experience, observations and reflections, abstract conceptualization and generalizations, or testing implications. Preferences for certain orientations influence, and are influenced by, courses and teachers, co-curricular activities, jobs, internships, and even the careers you enter. Choose activities that endeavor to strengthen each learning orientation so that they serve as tools for solving the problem situations you encounter.

Chapter 7 Relationships—at Home,
at Work, in the Community

- Post-graduation plans often create a separation between you and your family or long-time friends. This is a period when many new grads feel lonely and isolated; therefore, it is critical that you find the means and opportunities to remain connected to important people in your life.

- The learning curve that faces new graduates as they begin that "first job" is usually steep. In the first few weeks, your real job is to watch and listen in order to understand and acclimate to your work group. Discovering the sources of power, information, and special skills—as well as the norms that your co-workers live by—helps you determine the work style and behavior that will best suit you and the environment.

- Being an effective team member is key to success on the job. The skills inherent in being a good team player are: an ethical approach to tasks, taking initiative, keeping commitments, playing by the team rules, working diligently toward team goals, willingness to be cooperative and collaborative, sharing ideas and feedback constructively, applauding the ideas and achievements of others, handling conflict directly and respectfully, attending to and encouraging others (Greenberg and Baron).

- Developing mentors at work and in the community is particularly important to your adjustment to life after college. Your mentors can help you learn about yourself and the world, take personal responsibility for your own life, and recognize and use your special gifts (McGuire).

- Becoming a person-in-community means you are connected (beyond your workplace) to people and organizations that challenge, support, and inspire you. Finding places in the larger world where you can be involved in something bigger than yourself is essential to finding meaning and meaningful relationships (Daloz, Keen, Keen, and Parks).

Chapter 8 Working to Your Heart's Content

- Your college major may set the tone for the world view you will develop as life goes on, but is only one of many factors that combine to create a satisfying work life. Other considerations are your values, skills, interests, passions, and life-style choice.

- Finding work you love doing takes time and energy. The answer will not "dawn on you" unless you actively involve yourself in a process of discovery. Options to help you in your search include: using a mentor, connecting with a career counselor, reading about decision-making and career choices, using the web for research, volunteering, and participating in a range of internships and temporary jobs.

- There are several theories on how people choose careers. Holland suggests that people are happiest in a job that matches their values, skills, and interests. Krumboltz maintains that biology and environmental factors play a role—as does chance. Bordin believes that, while biography is the determining factor in career choice, you should also be looking for a job that fuses work and play. Understanding yourself from these varied perspectives is useful as you consider career possibilities.

■ The place you are called to is the place where your deep gladness and the world's deep hunger meet (Buechner). One of the tasks of young adulthood is to begin the discernment process that eventually brings your calling into the light. Living a meaningful life requires a "vision *of* yourself"—clear sense of identity—and a "vision *for* yourself"—clear sense of purpose. Connecting with people and activities that encourage your dreams and enlarge your sense of what is possible keeps you moving in the direction of your calling.

GOING WITH THE FLOW

Often college students looking toward graduation want to believe the lyrics of songwriter John Mayer when he sings, "*I just found out there's no such thing as the real world, just a lie you've got to rise above.*" New graduates, however, seem to believe that there is, in fact, a "real world"—a world that is as demanding as it is confusing. Nowhere are the demands and confusion as clear as they are in the first jobs of new college graduates. Many are bored and disappointed because the work is repetitive and uninspired, with no room for personal creativity. At the other extreme, others are terrified by their employers' expectations given the enormity of the learning curve that faces them. Still others, perhaps a minority, derive an exciting level of personal and professional satisfaction with their new work and quickly have optimal experiences. Since this book was written hoping that you would become, sooner or later, a member of the third group, one of the final concepts to be shared is an uplifting idea from positive psychology called "flow."

Flow is a term used to describe optimal experience; and, optimal experience is what most young professionals hope for from their jobs. Here are the common characteristics of optimal experience

> . . . a sense that one's skills are adequate to cope with the challenges at hand, in a goal-directed, rule-bound action system that provides clear clues as to how well one is performing. Concentration is so intense that there is no attention left over to think about anything irrelevant, or to worry about problems. Self-consciousness disappears, and the sense of time becomes distorted. An activity that produces such experiences is so gratifying that people are willing to do it for its own sake . . . (Csikszentmihalyi 1990, p. 71).

In the movie, *Billy Elliott,* Billy is asked what it feels like when he is dancing. He describes his experience by saying that he forgets everything and "sort of disappears." His whole body changes; he feels a fire inside. And there he is "flying—like a bird—like electricity." It is clear that when Billy is dancing, he is in flow. Throughout the movie, Billy demonstrates the eight features of flow. (1) His goals are clear—he wants nothing more in the world than to dance. (2) Feedback is immediate—his whole body changes. (3) There is a balance between opportunity and capacity—Billy has talent; his goal is to dance professionally. By moving to London and studying at the acclaimed Royal School of Ballet, he hopes to increase both his opportunities and his capacity as a dancer. (4) Concentration deepens—everything around him simply disappears. (5) The present is what matters—he is completely focused on the music and the dance he is doing in the moment. (6) Control is no problem—he keeps at the dance (the task at hand) even when he has difficulty with a new step. (7) The sense of time is altered—he flies until the music stops. (8) There is a loss of ego—he literally looses himself in the music. (Csikszentmihalyi 2003)

The athlete who has one of those "nothing but net" kind of games is experiencing flow. The situation allows the player to demonstrate a high level of skill while completely focused in a challenging, goal-directed, rule-bound action system called basketball. When you joyfully lose yourself and all sense of time in a challenging but attainable pastime—the New York Times crossword puzzle, planting a garden, reading, writing, remodeling a room—you are in flow. It is likely that you often experienced flow in school, e.g., writing a paper, researching for a project, listening to a particularly compelling speaker, playing in a band, participating in a demanding study group. If you were in flow, you became thoroughly engrossed in the task at hand and forgot about everything; you were surprised by how much time had passed or that time was up. Most important you were enjoying the process of applying your skills to the challenge you were facing; and, in so doing, you were feeling pretty good about yourself.

Building on Flow—The Stories of Jennifer and Ben

Flow can be such a common experience that you might not recognize it immediately. Jennifer, for instance, has had a lifelong love affair with words. A trip to a bookstore can take an afternoon—not because she plans it that way, but because she typically gets swept up in "browsing." When she finally emerges from the bookstore, she rushes home to begin reading one of her new purchases. She often finds herself waking up the next morning in the same spot she was reading in the night before. Jennifer might not include "reading" or "trips to the bookstore" on her list of peak experiences; yet, these everyday events put her in a state of flow.

Ben provides us with another example of finding flow in everyday places. At the beginning of his senior year, he became a volunteer at a community center in a Hispanic neighborhood. As a Spanish major, Ben saw it as an opportunity to hone his fluency. Ben worked in their after-school program, tutoring eight-to-ten-year-olds and supervising recreational activities. Soon, working with "his kids" was the best part of Ben's day. Ben is nearing graduation and it will be difficult to end what has become a flow experience.

CASE IN POINT 9.1   Rebecca Gets Her Flow Back

As an accounting major, Rebecca had done some research on specialties within the field. The area that really fascinated her was forensic accounting. Her "Plan A" became to find an experiential opportunity in this field. At the end of her sophomore year she interviewed for an internship with a forensic accounting firm that had a regional office in the same city in which she attended college. She happily accepted their offer and by mid-September she was getting hands-on experience in forensic accounting. The term ended, but Rebecca stayed on. In fact, she continued to work for the firm until graduation. She was in her element.

Several factors contributed to Rebecca's positive experience. She enjoyed applying the theory she was exposed to in school to real world problems. She was learning all the time. She also liked getting dressed up for work and going to a downtown office, laptop in hand. The single largest contributor to Rebecca's satisfaction with work however, was that the managing partner took notice of her talents, and he chose to mentor her.

The variety and level of challenge of her tasks insured that she was never bored; her mentor demanded a great deal of her. When he gave her an assignment, he expected her to wrestle with tough problems and to determine solutions. He was willing to answer questions and provide direction, but he never spoon-fed her. He always provided feedback in the form of praise or constructive criticism; either way, Rebecca was continuously honing her skills as an accountant and as an employee. Working directly with a partner and with clients, she was operating at a level that most new grads in accounting aspire to, and she was still a student. She didn't know it, but she had found flow in her work.

Rebecca graduated in 1998, a time when firms were offering signing bonuses to accounting majors. Her skills were in demand and she thought that she should at least see what else was out there. While she was encouraged by her mentor to do exactly that, he also prepared an offer and hiring package so Rebecca could have a base of comparison. In the end, she decided to take a position with a large consulting firm. Working in

---

How could Jennifer and Ben use their flow experiences to manage the transitions that face them?

_____

_____

How could these experiences help them make work–related choices?

_____

_____

How could these experiences inform their choices to build social and community ties?

_____

_____

CASE IN POINT 9.1   Continued

public accounting offered a certain amount of prestige, and it was less than 15 minutes from her home.

On her first day of work, she joined a large group of new hires for orientation. Her level of experience coming into the job didn't matter now. In the eyes of the people at this firm, she was just another new grad and needed to start at the beginning. She went from exciting and challenging assignments to small, rote tasks. She went from working hand-in-hand with the managing partner to a "frat house environment"—too many people who couldn't teach her anything and too much time on her hands. Rebecca reflected, "No matter how habitual I am in my personal life, I learned that I really need variety at work. I was used to being able to go directly to the person I needed in order to solve a problem; but, there (the consulting firm), approaching a partner to ask a question was considered inappropriate. The rules regarding chain of command were more important than doing good work. I hated going there and having nothing (of substance) to do."

Eventually the firm "discovered" her and went from giving her grunt work to sending her out on audits alone. There was no training and no one to give her feedback. Now she ricocheted from dull, mundane tasks to assignments for which she felt completely unprepared. She was an "unguided" missile and she knew it was not going to get any better. After six months, it was time to leave.

Rebecca returned to her former employer as a Staff Accountant III—not typical for a person who graduated from college just six months before. Five years later she is still there. Her job title and responsibilities have increased, and it is her turn to mentor new hires. The managing partner is also still there and still serves as her mentor sometimes, but the relationship is shifting to a more collegial one (see *Mentors for Your Career* in chapter 7). Her job continues to have all the elements of flow. She is drawn to it and challenged by it. She has the skill to do it well and continues to utilize her mentor's expertise. She works a lot but doesn't seem to mind it. She is happy and often in flow.

Understanding and learning to create flow can go a long way toward improving a young adult's self-esteem and post-graduation life-style. Flow creates opportunities to look ahead with happy anticipation rather than look back with longing. And now for the million dollar question—what do you do when there is no flow in your job, in your life? Look at Case in Point 9.1 to see how one new grad solved this problem.

Csikszentmihalyi's research brought to light an interesting and surprising finding—often people don't recognize flow when they are in it (1990). Perhaps it is because flow occurs without much fanfare. You can be in flow and never know it. Since your flow situations provide clues as to where an investment of your time and energy would have the greatest payoff for you in terms of personal satisfaction, we encourage you to recognize your own peak experiences. They are transformative moments that offer you important information about the quality of your endeavors and your life.

RECOGNIZING TRANSFORMATION

"Transformation," as defined by *Webster's Encyclopedic Unabridged Dictionary,* means "to change in condition, form, character, structure, nature; metamorphose." We tend to think of transformation as beautiful and amazing—caterpillar into butterfly—and its outcome certainly can be. But the process of transformation is usually very subtle or very messy. Either way it is a bit unnerving. Ask the caterpillar.

Think about the television show, *Trading Spaces,* as an example of the messy side of transformation. It derives its tremendous popularity from our fascination with the process of transformation. Now consider the *Trading Spaces* process. The designers are the "change agents." They sometimes lead and sometimes mentor the "transformation team" because they have a handle on the larger plan and trust their ability to make it happen. The "transformation team" usually has lots of questions, a tough time letting go of the old stuff, and difficulty choosing new colors, fabrics, and furniture.

The "transformation team" knows what they are getting into before they go on the show, yet they are exhausted and overwhelmed by the end of the first day. The room is torn apart with decorating tools and supplies everywhere. It's at this point that it is difficult to hang on to the vision of what the room will become. The whole process is pretty unnerving and someone invariably says that they won't get it done in time. Of course, they always do.

When we see the transformed room, it is usually a shock. It is the same room in the same house, yet it is completely different. It will take some time before the owners can walk into the room without thinking about it as "changed." In fact there is typically a lag in time between the completion of change and the integration of it into the fabric of life. The point at which they can walk into the room without feeling the change is the point as which the transformation is complete.

Some transformations happen quietly. They are practically imperceptible on a moment-to-moment basis. For instance, you can't watch your hair grow. Even though it is always growing, you don't notice that it has happened. One day you look in the mirror or see a picture of yourself from several months ago and recognize that your hair has gotten long. If you have worked to become fluent in another language, you will recognize the phenomenon that one day you realize that you are not only speaking the language but you are also thinking in it. Most people can't identify the exact moment when they fell in love—yet love is perhaps the most profound agent of transformation and proof that subtle transformations can also be unnerving.

Whether your transformations are noisy and chaotic or show up as faint undercurrents in your life, you will be transformed. As the essay at the beginning of this chapter suggests, there comes a time when—no matter how prepared you are—you have to let go and let the process guide you through the void. In some sense you are preparing to come to the spot that nothing can prepare you for—the place where you must leap and trust that the net will appear. True transformation requires coming to (looking before you leap)

CASE IN POINT 9.2   Drew's Transformation

Drew had worked as a student assistant in the student life office since his freshman year. In his last year of college, he had also served as a peer assistant for the area. Having come to his career choice a bit late, he hoped to attend graduate school immediately after completing his undergraduate education; however, his ability to carry out his plan depended on securing a graduate assistantship—preferably with student life.

Drew was encouraged by the student life staff to apply for the graduate program and for their assistantship. It was a win-win for everyone. He was offered and accepted the position in April. His graduate assistantship would begin the following August. In the meantime, he finished the semester, graduated in May, completed some prerequisites during the summer and worked, as always, as a student assistant in the student life office.

During his last two weeks as a student assistant, he began to make his graduate assistant space his own. He brought in a clock for the wall, hung some prints, and placed some pictures and personal items around his soon-to-be office. He left his student assistant position on a Friday and began his graduate assistant position the following Monday. He shopped over the weekend, replacing jeans and t-shirts with khakis and polos to fit in with the corporate casual look of the staff.

When he walked into the office that Monday, everything looked the same but everything felt different. Drew was now considered a part of the professional team, included in their meetings, their lunches, and their plans for the delivery of service to students. He was more than willing to tackle whatever tasks were given to him. He was doing his best to be the professional, but he secretly felt much more like the student he was just a few days before. It would take a while before Drew adapted to in his new role and began to think of himself as a staff member. Until then he would have to remind himself to head for his own office instead of the student desk when he walked through the door.

---

and moving through (leaping and the net will appear) that place. Our last case study, Case in Point 9.2, offers an example of a quiet, but nonetheless life-changing, transformation.

HAPPY BEGINNINGS

William Bridges said that transition begins with an ending, is followed by a limbo he calls the neutral zone, and ends in a new beginning. The authors of this book sincerely hope that

- you have begun your ending (long before graduation),
- you successfully navigate the unsettling uncertainties of the neutral zone, and
- your new beginnings are filled with flow.

We do not know who you are or what you will be doing in a few years, but we certainly wish you well on your journey through young adult life. Since it is your journey, we would appreciate receiving your feedback to the ideas and suggestions we presented. Your responses will enable us to update our knowledge of these issues for the benefit of other students. The publisher has provided a questionnaire at the end of the book for your feedback. Thank you and good luck!

JOURNAL STARTERS

1. To what extent do you identify with Danaan Parry's transition/trapeze metaphor? Why?

2. What do you think you will be doing professionally one or two years after graduation? Which three or four topics presented in the "A List" are most likely to help you through your transition?

3. Which experiences are most likely to put you in flow? What is the connection between these flow experiences and your calling?

4. Select one particular experience and trace the eight features of flow. Are they all represented? If not, what is missing?

5. During the last two years, what has been your most significant transformation?

REFERENCES

Csikszentmihalyi, M. (1990). *Flow*. New York, NY: Harper & Row.

Csikszentmihalyi, M. (2003). *Good business*. New York, NY: Viking Penguin.

Robbins, A. and Wilner, A. (2001). *Quarterlife crisis: The unique challenges of life in your twenties*. New York, NY: Jeremy P. Tarcher/Putnam.

Webster's encyclopedic unabridged dictionary. (1989). New York, NY: Gramercy Books.

Author Index

Adams, J. Stacy, 99, 160
Albion, Mark, 135, 154
Allen, James, 68
Anderson, N., 113
Arndt, T., 29, 31
Astin, Alexander, 11–12, 64, 70

Bandura, Albert, 97
Baron, R. A., 96, 99, 101, 113, 122–24, 126, 131, 161
Baxter Magolda, Marcia, 52–59, 64–65, 67–70, 74, 86, 93, 113, 128, 131, 159
Belenky, M. F., 69–70
Berdrow, I., 83–84, 88–89, 92, 160
Blimling, G. S., 68–70
Bolles, Richard, 154
Bordin, Edward, 144–45, 162
Braitman, Ellen, 90
Bridges, William, 2–4, 11–12, 14, 31, 79, 92, 167
Bryant, A., 68, 70
Buechner, Frederick, 146, 154, 162

Campbell, Joseph, 134
Caruso, D., 75, 92

Chickering, Arthur, 34, 39–43, 50, 75, 86, 158
Chouinard, Yvon, 129–30
Ciarrochi, J., 75–76, 78, 80, 92, 160
Clinchy, B. M., 69–70
Coelho, Paulo, 153–54
Cramer, C., 36, 50
Csikszentmihalyi, M., 119, 122, 126, 129, 131, 145, 162–63, 165, 168

Daloz, L. P., 126–27, 130–31, 161
Dixon, Nancy M., 93, 109–10, 113–14
Donovan, J. J., 97, 113
Douglass, Fredrick, 26

Edison, Thomas, 73
Emerson, Ralph Waldo, 94
Erikson, Erik, 35–37, 43
Evans, N. J., 35, 50
Evers, F. T., 83–85, 88–89, 92, 160

Fisher, Anne, 139, 154
Fisher, Cynthia, 21
Flynn, B., 36, 50
Folsom, Byron, 20, 32
Foreman, Robert, 20, 31

Subject Index

TO THE OWNER OF THIS BOOK:

I hope that you have found Connect College to Career, first edition, useful. So that this book can be improved in a future edition, would you take the time to complete this sheet and return it? Thank you.

School and address: _____

_____

Department: _____

Instructor's name: _____

1. What I like most about this book is: _____

_____

_____

2. What I like least about this book is: _____

_____

_____

3. My general reaction to this book is: _____

_____

_____

4. The name of the course in which I used this book is: _____

_____

5. Were all of the chapters of the book assigned for you to read? _____

   If not, which ones weren't? _____

6. In the space below, or on a separate sheet of paper, please write specific suggestions for improving this book and anything else you'd care to share about your experience in using this book.

_____

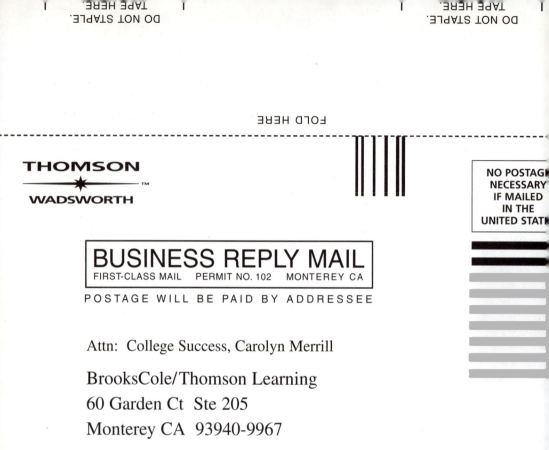

THOMSON
™
WADSWORTH

BUSINESS REPLY MAIL
FIRST-CLASS MAIL   PERMIT NO. 102   MONTEREY CA

POSTAGE WILL BE PAID BY ADDRESSEE

Attn: College Success, Carolyn Merrill

BrooksCole/Thomson Learning
60 Garden Ct Ste 205
Monterey CA 93940-9967

OPTIONAL:

Your name:_____ Date: _____

May we quote you, either in promotion for Connect College to Career,
First edition, or in future publishing ventures?

Yes: _____ No: _____

Sincerely yours,

Paul Hettich
Camille Helkowski